Here to There

So It's Time to Change Churches?

Doug Burrier

Here to There
So It's Time to Change Churches?
by Doug Burrier

Printed in the United States of America

ISBN 978-1-60477-751-2

doug.burrier@servant*driven*.org
Founder and President
© 2006, 2007, 2008 All Rights Reserved Doug Burrier
Servant*Driven* is a trademark of Doug Burrier

www.xulonpress.com

Here to There

So It's Time to Change Churches?

Doug Burrier

It is better to wait forever to make the correct decision than to live forever with the wrong decision.

We can expect that God will either call us to leave or we will encounter others leaving our local church. We need to be prepared to leave well (or help our friends leave well) long before the departure.

The truths in these pages will be most profitable to the one who is not even thinking about leaving. After all, you have to live well among the believers at your church before you can leave well. The truths in this book explore much about what we should and should not be expecting and experiencing as we gather together as believers.

If you are ready to leave, you might want to pause, continue reading, and allow knowledge about leaving well to percolate into wisdom before you leave. After all, you would not want to leave if there might be something you don't know about living and leaving well.

No matter your circumstance, it's time that we do whatever we can to stop the flow of poor departures that divide the body of Christ. It's time that believers stand together, defeat the enemy, and keep the glory for our God.

Table of Contents

Chapter 1

So You Are Ready to Change Churches
Are You Sure God Is Ready?

If God tells you to leave, you need to leave, and the church needs to love you and champion your departure. Some departures, though perhaps surrounded in sorrow, are easy for everyone to process.

Take the geographical move, for example. This move is based on simple logic. God told someone to move to a new town, and now he must move to a new local church. Saying goodbye is tearful, difficult, and sad, but it is not stressful. Everyone prayed with him about the job change or the move, and now it is time to say, "Goodbye."

Things are just as easy when people move following God into ministry. A fellow member's departure to go work for God may be sad or difficult, but the departure is seen in the light of success. There are going-away parties, commissioning services, and people stand taller with great pride in the work of God in their church. After all, a healthy church dreams of having people go into ministry.

Departures for poor reasons, however, are difficult. When people give up on their family, departures are difficult. Everyone knows something is not right. Those left behind in a poor departure may feel inadequate. They may be hurt because they still hoped and loved. Likewise, the person leaving may be hurt. Some may be angry or, even worse, indifferent. Everyone loses in a poor departure because the gift of love did not grow into something greater, stronger, or better.

Everyone has seen God move godly people in righteous ways to new ministries and places. What is the difference between leaving poorly and leaving well? Who leaves poorly, and who leaves well? What are they like? There are many differences between these two groups of people, but there is one simple answer.

Those who leave well leave because God clearly said, "Go there!" When God calls, man needs to answer but whether or not a man is prepared to leave well will be determined long before God calls him to go. Those that leave well have lived well among the church long before leaving well.

God saying "Go" and "there" is important to understand. A person who leaves well from a healthy church will be blessed as he sees his church family confirm God's direction. He will have seen himself as part of the local body of Christ. He will have shared his prayer, his passion, and the pain of even thinking of leaving with leadership and the church. They will have joined him in prayer. The person who leaves well from an unhealthy church may not see such a supportive departure, but he will still be certain that God said "Go." He will still have tried to seek the anointing of the leaders and the church. Those who leave well leave because God told them to leave and they also know where they are going.

Many people leave claiming to be called on an Abraham journey. These people often say that God has told them to go but not told them where. "We aren't sure why. We just feel the need to look around," they say as they wander away. However, to assert that Abraham, and, other church fathers, did not know where they were going is biblically inaccurate.

God told each of those men exactly where to go each day along the way. Where in the Bible did God say, "Go find a better land. Wander. I will let you know when you find it. Go find something you like"? God is not in the wandering business. He is in the directing business.

The greatest example of biblical wandering is the saddest example of wandering. The people of God wandered in the desert for forty years because they did not like the "church" of the new land. They did not want to do what took faith. They did not want to finish what God told them to do. They did not understand God's purpose for them. They bailed out before the work was done; they just wanted a break, to rest and to relax. Interestingly, these people got their wish and died without ever seeing the land and blessings God wanted for them. Many believers claim that God is their guide but live as if He is only supposed to confirm their personal plans. Those who leave well leave because God has told them, "Go there!", and they have lived well before leaving.

Leaving poorly simply moves immature people from place to place. Attending a church is about being a part of a family of God. Attending will always be about striving together, growing together, loving together, and living together. Being a part of a church means resolving all your difficulties and getting answers to all your questions. Living as a church means believing in one another and staying to the end. Leaving poorly is about the one leaving. Leaving well is about God. He is, after all, the one great reason to leave.

Leaving is better when everyone is involved and sees that the ones leaving are on a mission from God. Leaving well brings tears of separation but joy for the journey that is about to happen. Leaving well does not separate and divide the church but spreads and shares the church. Leaving well affirms accountability to the fellowship of a local church. Leaving well respects the people of God. Christ's church grows stronger with every good and holy departure. After all, there is only one great reason to leave—because God said "Go there!"

Neither the church nor the individual should stand in the way of such a departure, for they will find themselves standing in the face of God. God wants us to leave for the one great reason. God wants to lead us to a place where we will live well long before, if ever, we are called to leave well.

God will call believers to change churches, and they need to leave well with the love and blessing of their church. Unfortunately, many departures are poor departures because of the reason or the method of departure. Many of those leaving poorly are not even aware that they are settling for less than the best of God. Unfortunately, aware or unaware, each believer leaving poorly remains accountable for his actions and suffers the consequences of bad reason or ignorance. Many churches are not places where believers can live well or from which believers can leave well.

It is time that Christians do whatever they can to stop the flow of poor departures that divide the body of Christ. It is time that believers stand together, defeat the enemy, and keep the glory for God.

People Are Changing Churches

Millions of people join evangelical churches every year. Tremendous growth is reported. Christian resources are published by the millions and are more available than at any time in history. It seems that Christianity is absolutely growing through the roof. These are exciting days, as Christianity enjoys a growing popularity with the press and mega-churches draw attention as contemporary and culturally relevant institutions. One would think that entire cities would be transformed and that the nation would be revived for Christ. However, despite the reports, the church is left asking, "Wait a minute. Where are those millions of additions to the church?"

The statistics of church growth are easily misunderstood; the results are being poorly interpreted and even more poorly presented. Millions of people are joining evangelical churches each year, but some 80 percent of these new members simply transferred from one church to another church. The "church swap" accounts for the vast majority of the annual reports of growth.

There are a few mega-churches, which, with great momentum, claim that 50 percent or more of their growth came from new converts to the faith. There are a few movements worldwide where people under oppression are hearing and responding to the gospel by the thousands. However, most reported church growth is only the growth of one church at the loss of another church. It is not true growth; it is just coming and going. The question remains, "Were all those people supposed to change churches? Did they leave well because God told them to leave?"

People Are Disappearing

Do you remember the big search for the Georgia woman who disappeared right before her wedding? She fled because she got cold feet. She let her family live through the horror of thinking she was dead. She let her neighbors, friends, and thousands of volunteers search while she hid in a hotel. In the end, she was despised, condemned, and charged with a crime. People were astonished, unbelieving at first. Some tried to be compassionate, while most simply made fun of her. Time passed, and the majority of people do not even remember her name.

In the same way, thousands of people leave the church every year. They disappear with no explanation or notification. Some churches hunt for them, and other churches don't

search for them. Few of these people ever offer up an explanation to their ex-leaders or ex-church members. Sometimes
ignorantly and other times not, many people leave the way
the missing bride did—selfishly and never understanding
the responsibilities and love of a real family. These people
don't take their vows seriously. They don't understand
commitment.

People Leave Because of Personal Problems

There are very real people leaving the church. They are
friends, companions, and acquaintances. Many of them are
leaving for personal problems. They leave and never say
goodbye. They leave behind church families destined to
hear bits and pieces about why they left without being given
the honor owed to brothers and sisters. These people leave
differently yet with personal problems hindering a good
departure. They leave claiming that they:

- Do not agree with leadership at some point.
- Outgrew the ability to learn and needed to do their
  own thing.
- Could not get into the new groove or were disillusioned.
- Sinned and could not stand staying.
- Did not care anymore.
- Were told to leave.
- Were embarrassed.

Many of these people are involved right up to the moment
of their departure. They stand up to be heard in meetings, at
classes, and as leaders. They have no problem saying, "Take
me as a member—I am committed," but not one of them
says, "Goodbye." They leave quietly. They leave noisily.
They leave for personal reasons, and they do not leave well.

Leaving saying, "It is me, not you," is like using a poor breakup line on a boyfriend or girlfriend. Leaving quietly does not ensure leaving in a healthy way. Personal problems need to be resolved before people separate.

> And now I want to plead with those two women, Euodia and Syntyche. Please, because you belong to the Lord, settle your disagreement. And I ask you, my true teammate, to help these women, for they worked hard with me in telling others the Good News. And they worked with Clement and the rest of my co-workers, whose names are written in the Book of Life.—Phil. 4:2-3 (NLT)

People leaving for personal reasons do not understand the commitment of Christians to the church. They do not understand how to live well together.

People Settle for Less Than the Best

Some people disappear intentionally or unintentionally, but others simply take what they can get. Countless people settle for everything from missing God's best to intentionally disobeying God. Do you remember the Reubenites, the Gadites, and the half tribe of Manasseh? Their history is amazing.

> Now the tribes of Reuben and Gad owned vast numbers of livestock. So when they saw that the lands of Jazer and Gilead were ideally suited for their flocks and herds, they came to Moses, Eleazar the priest, and the other leaders of the people. They said, "Ataroth, Dibon, Jazer, Nimrah, Heshbon, Elealeh, Sebam, Nebo, and Beon—the LORD has conquered this whole area for the people of Israel. It is ideally

suited for all our flocks and herds. If we have found favor with you, please let us have this land as our property instead of giving us land across the Jordan River."

"Do you mean you want to stay back here while your brothers go across and do all the fighting?"... But they responded to Moses, "We simply want to build sheepfolds for our flocks and fortified cities for our wives and children. Then we will arm ourselves and lead our fellow Israelites into battle until we have brought them safely to their inheritance. Meanwhile, our families will stay in the fortified cities we build here, so they will be safe from any attacks by the local people...We would rather live here on the east side where we have received our inheritance." Then Moses said, "If you keep your word and arm yourselves for the LORD's battles...And the land on the east side of the Jordan will be your inheritance from the LORD...Go ahead and build towns for your families and sheepfolds for your flocks, but do everything you have said." — Num. 32:1-24 (NLT)

These people of God gave up God's chosen land for a land that looked great at the time. A logical question arises: Why would anyone settle for less than God's best for them? Many times, people settle because they don't understand the ways, the heart, or the plans of God. Many times people simply want immediate gratification, so they choose what seems expediently good rather than what is best over time. Esau is a great example. He was hungry one day and sold his future to satisfy his momentary hunger:

One day when Jacob was cooking some stew, Esau arrived home exhausted and hungry from a hunt. Esau said to Jacob, "I'm starved! Give me some of that red stew you've made." (This was how Esau got his other name, Edom—"Red.")

Jacob replied, "All right, but trade me your birthright for it."

"Look, I'm dying of starvation!" said Esau. "What good is my birthright to me now?"

So Jacob insisted, "Well then, swear to me right now that it is mine." So Esau swore an oath, thereby selling all his rights as the firstborn to his younger brother. Then Jacob gave Esau some bread and lentil stew. Esau ate and drank and went on about his business, indifferent to the fact that he had given up his birthright.—Gen. 25:29-34 (NLT)

Like so many young people, Esau lived in the "now" and did not understand the implications of giving up what would benefit him in the future for what would benefit him at the moment. Who could believe that Esau would have really died if he'd had to wait to cook his own food? Esau's poor rationalization led him to make a grave error. Both of these histories illustrate people making poor decisions and settling for less than they should have received from God. Even worse, their shortsighted, personally focused actions had far-reaching implications on future generations. The long run is not always easy, pretty, or simple, but he who perseveres wins the prize.

I press on toward the goal for the prize of the upward call of God in Christ Jesus.—Phil. 3:14

Blessed is a man who perseveres under trial; for once he has been approved, he will receive the crown of life which the Lord has promised to those who love Him.—James 1:12

People who leave well invest in long-term success. People who leave poorly settle for less. People who leave well understand a fellowship commitment. People who leave poorly do not understand the commitments that healthy family members make to one another, and they don't truly make these commitments. Relationships take long-term commitment. Living well together takes work.

Pay close attention to yourself and to your teaching; persevere in these things, for as you do this you will ensure salvation both for yourself and for those who hear you. — 1 Tim. 4:16

Living well together is the long-term investment that allows the church to claim all of the promises of peace, happiness, and success. Settling divides the church and steals its strength.

The Church Has a Responsibility

Christians have a responsibility to leave well and are accountable when they settle for less than a strong, great departure. In the same way, the church has a responsibility. The church has the responsibility to teach people the biblical truths regarding church life, living well together, and not violating the fellowship. The church also needs to be careful not to judge or try to stop those who are thinking of leaving the church. Even when someone is in the middle of disappearing, the church needs to remember the story of Gamaliel and be careful before intervening.

The apostles were teaching about Jesus when the Jewish leaders had them arrested. Gamaliel, a Jewish leader and teacher, was at their trial.

"Didn't we tell you never again to teach in this man's name?" the high priest demanded. "Instead, you have filled all Jerusalem with your teaching about Jesus, and you intend to blame us for his death!" But Peter and the apostles replied, "We must obey God rather than human authority. The God of our ancestors raised Jesus from the dead after you killed him by crucifying him. Then God put him in the place of honor at his right hand as Prince and Savior. He did this to give the people of Israel an opportunity to turn from their sins and turn to God so their sins would be forgiven. We are witnesses of these things and so is the Holy Spirit, who is given by God to those who obey him."

At this, the high council was furious and decided to kill them. But one member had a different perspective.

He was a Pharisee named Gamaliel, who was an expert on religious law and was very popular with the people. He stood up and ordered that the apostles be sent outside the council chamber for a while. Then he addressed his colleagues as follows: "Men of Israel, take care what you are planning to do to these men! Some time ago there was that fellow Theudas, who pretended to be someone great. About four hundred others joined him, but he was killed, and his followers went their various ways. The whole movement came to nothing. After him, at the time of the census, there was Judas of Galilee. He got some people to follow him, but he was killed, too, and all his followers were scattered.

"So my advice is, leave these men alone. If they are teaching and doing these things merely on their own, it will soon be overthrown. But if it is of God, you will not be able to stop them. You may even find yourselves fighting against God." — Acts 5:28-39 (NLT)

Church leaders and members often think that they know the plan of God for everyone. The church doesn't need to focus on stopping someone who claims, "This is of God!" Time will tell everything. Instead of interrupting what God may be doing in their life, the church needs to challenge them to leave well — saving their character, uniting the church, and honoring God. If someone can leave well, then God is glorified and His will is accomplished. If they don't choose to leave well, they will leave anyway.

The church needs to love those that leave poorly as much as it loves those that leave well. Those that leave poorly don't need to be disliked, distrusted, or hated. They need unconditional love, prayer, and grace. Their departure should be mourned, because the enemy has once again gotten the church to settle for less than the best.

Nonetheless, the church must accept and understand that a local church is not the complete church. The church is made up of all believers, everywhere. The geographic location of a believer is not the concern of men but of God. The church and every believer should simply desire that people are where God wants them to be and are doing His work there. A local church should not try be performance-oriented based on its size or the duration of its members. The performance of the local church should be based on the same standard as the church overall. The church is healthy when the people are living well.

Good Reasons and Good Departures

People can leave well for very good reasons.

People are going to leave. Many of them will leave for a good reason, with God's blessing. There are good reasons to change churches. When God takes a good reason and tells the believer "Go there!" the good reason has just become one great reason to leave. All that remains is for the believer to leave well.

Leaving is not the problem; it is why and how people leave that can be the problem. Christians need to leave well when they leave a local church. Christians need to live with a great commitment to fellowship. Christians need to avoid the common cost to all who leave poorly — missing out on what God intended for them in the long run. The long run is not always easy, pretty, or simple, but he who perseveres wins the prize.

It is time for Christians to be the church. It is time that believers do whatever they can to stop the flow of poor departures that divide the body of Christ. It is time that believers stand together, defeat the enemy, and return glory to God. It is time for believers to be happy together and apart. It is time for believers to live well and learn well at home before they ever think about leaving.

Chapter 2

Ten Good Reasons to Leave

A key piece of knowledge on the subject of leaving a church is this:

There are good reasons to leave a church.

The point has been iterated and needs to be reiterated here—there are good reasons to leave. The issue is not leaving but leaving well. Christians should be defined by succeeding to do "all things unto the glory of God"—even when it comes to leaving their church.

There are good reasons to go to another church, but there is never a reason good enough to leave the church overall. The true believer who sits at home instead of assembling, identifying, and serving with the church finds himself convicted of a crime before God.

And let us not neglect our meeting together—Heb. 10:25 (NLT)

Any plan of departure that involves leaving the overall church for any period of time is a flawed plan. Pastors and congregation members who see departure in a negative light need to begin accepting that there are good reasons to leave a church. Here are ten of those good reasons.

1. The Church Is Doctrinally Unsound

A doctrinally unsound church is dangerous, misleading, and oppressive. Countless Christians have been misled, misguided, and hurt in the midst of believers and leaders in doctrinally unsound churches. The damage caused by doctrinally unsound churches is a travesty, and the people who support those churches are not righteous.

> So if we say we have fellowship with God, but we continue living in darkness, we are liars and do not follow the truth. But if we live in the light, as God is in the light, we can share fellowship with each other... Anyone who says, "I know God," but does not obey God's commands is a liar, and the truth is not in that person. But if someone obeys God's teaching, then in that person God's love has truly reached its goal. This is how we can be sure we are living in God: Whoever says that he lives in God must live as Jesus lived. — 1 John 1:6-2:6 (NCV)

Every person has the right—better even, the responsibility—to expect and be part of a doctrinally sound church. God requires leaders to be held accountable to maintain a doctrinally sound church. God commands Christians to only choose doctrinally sound churches.

> Do not be bound together with unbelievers; for what partnership have righteousness and lawlessness, or what fellowship has light with darkness? — 2 Cor. 6:14

When Christians invest the time, money, and talents that God has given them to invest, they are to invest with righteous, lawful people who are full of God's light. Believers are called by God to have a high standard—a biblical standard—when picking friends, churches, spouses, and ministries. We simply must demand righteousness in intimate and important relationships.

So when it comes to our church and our doctrine, we must demand that our church be doctrinally sound. But what is unsound doctrine? How can unsound doctrine be identified and avoided?

The only way to identify unsound doctrine is to know sound doctrine. The only way to know if a truth is not biblical is to know biblical truth. Unfortunately, many people aren't confident about their biblical knowledge and when asked, "What is sound doctrine?" defer to church leadership saying, "They are the leaders, and they are responsible to determine good doctrine and to hear from God." There are also people who believe that no one leader can determine sound doctrine and that the entire body must decide. However, defining sound doctrine requires neither deferring nor democracy. Doctrine can be defined as:

A belief or set of beliefs held and taught by a political party, group or church.

Christians' doctrine should be the set of beliefs from the Bible, since the very definition of a Christian is found in the Bible. Can different Christians have different doctrine? Any outsider, any scientist, any reasonably thinking person can conclude that if the Bible defines a Christian, then there can only be one doctrine of a Christian. If the Bible gives more than one possible definition of Christianity, the entire foundation crumbles and leaves no Christianity—much less, any Christian doctrine.

The Bible is the only way to determine Christian doctrine since it is the only objective, impersonal record of God's revealed words on the subject. The Bible is full of instruction regarding the who, what, when, where, why, and how of teaching and following God. The Bible is the basis for all sound Christian doctrine. Any Christian doctrine should be able to stand the test of consistency with the whole of the Bible. The Bible is simple and clear. The doctrines are also simple, clear, and easy to identify.

Doctrines are not actions but beliefs. Many people equate "sound doctrine" with doing what God wants done, teaching what God wants taught and making decisions God's way. Unsound beliefs (doctrine) will result in unsound choices and actions, but doctrines are not actions. Church doctrine is the set of beliefs held by the church as a whole. In the mainstream of Christianity, the stated and written church beliefs do not usually change and do not usually contradict the Bible. The person desiring to leave a church because of unsound doctrine should challenge himself by asking, "If the stated or written beliefs of the church have not changed since my arrival, should I have checked out the beliefs a little more diligently before binding myself to ungodliness?" If he chooses to leave, he needs to learn from his mistake and check the stated and written doctrine of his new church before making any commitments.

If people are going to leave a church because it has unsound doctrine, they must first know what sound doctrine is. They must know the beliefs of the church and be able to demonstrate that those beliefs (not the actions) are in error according to God and the Bible. If the church's stated beliefs are in opposition to or not consistent with the Bible, then there is good reason to leave the church.

2. The Church Is Ignoring the Truth

> The teachers of religious law and the Pharisees are
> the official interpreters of the Scriptures. So prac-
> tice and obey whatever they say to you, but don't
> follow their example. For they don't practice what
> they teach. They crush you with impossible reli-
> gious demands and never lift a finger to help ease the
> burden. — Matt. 23:2-4 (NLT)

When a church knows the truth (has good doctrine) but
fails to follow what it claims to be true, it ignores the truth.
Hypocrisy (saying one thing and doing another) is foolish
and embarrassing to the church, but there is an even greater
cost to be paid by the next generation of believers.

The Bible gives a good picture of people who believed
the right thing but long since stopped doing the right thing.
These leaders (and people) kept up appearances, said the
right things, and wrote the right thing, but behind it all they
were hypocrites.

> Yes, woe upon you, Pharisees, and you other reli-
> gious leaders-hypocrites! For you tithe down to the
> last mint leaf in your garden, but ignore the important
> things-justice and mercy and faith. Yes, you should
> tithe, but you shouldn't leave the more important
> things undone. Blind guides! You strain out a gnat
> and swallow a camel.
> Woe to you, Pharisees, and you religious leaders—
> hypocrites! You are so careful to polish the outside
> of the cup, but the inside is foul with extortion and
> greed. Blind Pharisees! First cleanse the inside of the
> cup, and then the whole cup will be clean.
> Woe to you, Pharisees, and you religious leaders!
> You are like beautiful mausoleums-full of dead

men's bones, and of foulness and corruption. You try to look like saintly men, but underneath those pious robes of yours are hearts besmirched with every sort of hypocrisy and sin.—Matt. 23:23-28 (TLB)

God's message to them is God's message to us and to today's church. "Woe" to us if we are hypocrites or if we bind ourselves to hypocrites. The empty life of saying one thing and doing another is not healthy for us or our families. And a church that ignores the truth is doomed to wander from God.

A hypocritical environment starves a growing believer because he hears what to do but has no example to follow. He finds himself challenged with wanting to believe but trying to figure out why he should do what the church doesn't do. In a short time, the growing believer will have to choose a life of frustration or a change of location.

Mature believers in a hypocritical church quickly become frustrated, concerned, heartbroken, sad, and uncomfortable. The mature believer can choose to depart, but if he stays, he will have to live the life of a prophet or surrender his maturity. The Bible is clear that the mature believer must be a responsible watchman for his family:

Son of man, speak to your people and tell them: Suppose I bring the sword against a land, and the people of that land select a man from among them, appointing him as their watchman, and he sees the sword coming against the land and blows his trumpet to warn the people. Then, if anyone hears the sound of the trumpet but ignores the warning, and the sword comes and takes him away, his blood will be on his own head. Since he heard the sound of the trumpet but ignored the warning, his blood is on his own hands. If he had taken warning, he would have saved his life. However, if the watchman sees the sword coming but doesn't blow the trumpet, so that the people aren't warned, and the sword comes and takes away their lives, then they have been taken away because of their iniquity, but I will hold the watchman accountable for their blood. — Ezek. 33:2-6 (HCSB)

The mature leader must begin to call the people back to God. The mature follower must warn his brothers and sisters of their collective foolishness and light a path for change. No matter how lonely the path, the mature believers in a hypocritical church must take on the duty of brother saving brother at the cost of their own lives.

My dear brothers and sisters, if anyone among you wanders away from the truth and is brought back again, you can be sure that the one who brings that person back will save that sinner from death and bring about the forgiveness of many sins. — James 5:19-20 (NLT)

When a church ignores the truth, the immature should leave immediately. The growing will probably have to leave as well. The mature will have to ask their Father, "Have I done everything that I can do to help revive the church, to light a path to change, to help save the innocent?" The mature have to fulfill their role, as long as necessary, remaining until they are ready to leave their church condemned and having no one cry "Truth!" among them.

3. The Church Is Dead

A dead church steals your joy, your soul, your heart, and the essence of your life. Dead churches are morgues full of seemingly content corpses stored in drawers. Everything seems okay until the drawers are opened and the people must work together; then a stench arises. The dead church ruins Christianity for everyone.

> The One who has the seven spirits and the seven stars says this: I know what you do. People say that you are alive, but really you are dead. Wake up! Make yourselves stronger before what you have left dies completely. I have found that what you are doing is less than what my God wants. So do not forget what you have received and heard. Obey it, and change your hearts and lives. So you must wake up, or I will come like a thief, and you will not know when I will come to you.—Rev. 3:1-3 (NCV)

"The church is dead" is an incredibly good reason to leave, but there are some interesting thoughts surrounding such a justifiable departure. How does a church die? What does it mean to be a dead church?

Why would a sold-out believer join a dead church unless God called him to join it? If he joined it knowing it was a dead church and because of God, then he has a job to do. His job is to reach the church, wake it up, and breathe life into it. His work will be empowered by God because of God's call until the work is over.

However, most believers in a dead church find themselves guilty of joining that fellowship while they were dead as well. They have woken up in their own spirituality and come alive. The "waking up" believer understands how horrible it is to be dead. Think about it. If you woke up in a morgue, next to dead, rotting people, would you want to stay or go? You would want to leave—especially if you had just come back from the dead! The waking-up believer needs to pause before he runs out of the front door of his dead church.

He needs to realize that the same zeal that makes him want to run away should be channeled into evangelism. His testimony to the new life that God has given may be the needed call to revive his dead church home. The awakened believer could be the spark that lights the fire. He may be the very tool used by God to bring back life to what was dead. The task might be scary; it might be daunting; it might be unpopular; but with love and a call to life, the awakened believer must testify before he leaves. If his message is not heard, then like the disciples of old, he will sadly find himself free to go.

> But whatever city you enter and they do not receive you, go out into its streets and say, "Even the dust of your city which clings to our feet we wipe off in protest against you; yet be sure of this, that the kingdom of God has come near."—Luke 10:10-11

4. The Church Just Isn't a Good Match

Why do people stay where they don't feel a match? Some stay because they simply don't like change, while others stay because of the few connections that they experience. Some people endlessly hope for things to get better—always hoping.

But every churchgoing person knows how horrible it is to live in a church fellowship where they don't feel like they are a part of the plan. When you are trapped in a church where you don't feel like you belong, you never get the fellowship that you really need. Christianity is a team sport and not a solo adventure. Those who have read the Bible know that fellowship, family, and a "nation" mentality are what make the followers of God strong, resilient, and confident. It is this identity that keeps the faith going generation after generation while the body purifies and guards itself.

> Therefore encourage one another and build up one another, just as you also are doing...Live in peace with one another. — 1 Thess. 5:11-13

How can an outsider find the fullness of God that's intended to be found in the fellowship? It would be better for him to find a church of better fit and to be part of the fellowship there. Unfortunately, so many of those people who find themselves not feeling a part of the party often miss one or two critical truths about loneliness.

- The ones who don't feel a part of the plan need to be proactive (after all, they have fellowship responsibilities too). They need to try to connect with people, accept invitations to dinner and service, and be willing to start a conversation.
- The ones who don't feel like the church is a good match need to ask, "Why did God bring me here?" As Christians mature, they usually find that God does not move them to a ministry so that they will feel something but rather so that they will find something and give something.

In life, if the outsider tries, he will eventually find himself in a conversation. Someone else is probably getting bored or lonely. Finding people, taking a risk, or getting involved in a silly party game is all it usually takes to turn a flop into an event of new friends and fun. The Lord expects Christians to seek out one another, to connect, to encourage, and not to discriminate. The outsider is often the one who is discriminating by not giving the others opportunity.

> Be devoted to one another in brotherly love; give preference to one another in honor; not lagging behind in diligence, fervent in spirit, serving the

Lord; rejoicing in hope, persevering in tribulation, devoted to prayer, contributing to the needs of the saints, practicing hospitality.

Bless those who persecute you; bless and do not curse. Rejoice with those who rejoice, and weep with those who weep. Be of the same mind toward one another; do not be haughty in mind, but associate with the lowly. Do not be wise in your own estimation. Never pay back evil for evil to anyone. Respect what is right in the sight of all men. If possible, so far as it depends on you, be at peace with all men. — Rom. 12:10-18

Believers are called to reach out to and be a part of all believers' lives. All believers are called to devotion, to give preference, to contribute, and to be involved with all believers—that is, all kinds of believers. This is the beauty of the variety of the body of Christ.

The focus of fellowship living is the One who invited everyone to the party. He wants you to meet the other guests. He wants believers to be proactive—even if the others are shy. He wants everyone to be part of the body of Christ at a local level.

Now may the God who gives perseverance and encouragement grant you to be of the same mind with one another according to Christ Jesus, so that with one accord you may with one voice glorify the God and Father of our Lord Jesus Christ. Therefore, accept one another, just as Christ also accepted us to the glory of God. — Rom. 15:5-7

With all of this said, if a church truly isn't a good fit, it may be best to leave. Before going, though, ask and answer, "How did I end up in a place where I didn't fit in?" The answer to this question will help you find that "fit" in the next church. Just make sure you are not making fellowship life all about your life instead of God's desires for you. Sometimes believers don't seem like a good match because God is using them to broaden each other.

5. The Church Has Too Much To Say

Some churches seem to make life difficult for people as they try to follow God. How many believers have said, "Every time I get a great idea, feel called by God, or get excited, someone pours cold water on me" or "Does everything have to be done their way?" or "Do they have to control every little thing?" A church not open to God moving in ways unfamiliar to the establishment can feel, and sometimes be, oppressive. Justifying every little uniqueness of how God created you or called you to be can be demanding. To have people say, "That just isn't the way we do it here" when you share you life or biblical calling can be discouraging. The church criticizing your biblical walk with God is a good reason to leave a church.

Church is truly a corporate effort. The church is a cooperative of people working as a team to glorify God, to worship Him, and to serve Him. However, living as children of God has both corporate and individual components because the church is comprised of individual Christians coming together for corporate purposes. There is no mandate preventing an individual from having personal callings that are not consistent with another's individual calling.

Think about Paul and Barnabas and their great evangelistic work among the Gentiles. Paul was called from the moment of his salvation to preach freedom — not law — to the Gentiles.

But the Lord said to him, "Go, for he is a chosen instrument of Mine, to bear My name before the Gentiles and kings and the sons of Israel; for I will show him how much he must suffer for My name's sake."—Acts 9:15-16

Paul and Barnabas saw great success in the Spirit as they reached out to the lost Gentiles and saw thousands come to believe in Jesus Christ. When they came back to their home church in Jerusalem, a debate ensued with those focusing on the salvation of the Jews; it was an argument of being fair and just, an argument of corporate living. However, Peter understood the difference in ministry and people:

When they arrived in Jerusalem, Paul and Barnabas were welcomed by the whole church, including the apostles and elders. They reported on what God had been doing through their ministry. But then some of the men who had been Pharisees before their conversion stood up and declared that all Gentile converts must be circumcised and be required to follow the law of Moses.

So the apostles and church elders got together to decide this question. At the meeting, after a long discussion, Peter stood and addressed them as follows: "Brothers, you all know that God chose me from among you some time ago to preach to the Gentiles so that they could hear the Good News and believe. God, who knows people's hearts, confirmed that he accepts Gentiles by giving them the Holy Spirit, just as he gave him to us. He made no distinction between us and them, for he also cleansed their hearts through faith. Why are you now questioning God's way by burdening the Gentile believers with a yoke that neither we nor our ancestors were able to bear? We believe that we are all saved the same way, by the special favor of the Lord Jesus." — Acts 15:3-11 (NLT)

Peter was wise in the Spirit of God. He knew that no one had been or would ever be able to keep the entire law of God. He knew that Jesus came to set men free by fulfilling the law and being a sacrifice for all sin. Believers were still to follow God's principles, but Peter realized that Jesus did not come to make Gentiles into Jews; Jesus came to make believers of all those who would believe. The Gentiles would have a different social walk with Jesus than the Jews and did not need to be burdened with having to live Christianity as a Jew.

In essence, Peter said to the council, "Let these people live their calling as Christians. They are not Jews but they are believers just like those who are Jews. Do not say so much to them. Don't discourage them."

Christians not only have different cultures and work with different groups, but they also have different callings in those cultures and groups. The Bible is clear that even leaders are called to do different tasks for the kingdom of God.

And He gave some as apostles, and some as prophets, and some as evangelists, and some as pastors and teachers. — Eph. 4:11

If the church has too much to say about your life — discouraging you in your walk, call, and ministry rather than encouraging and championing — it might be time for you to find a fellowship that is healthy. However, be certain that their discouragement is really discouragement.

Sometimes what a younger believer sees as discouragement is simply a mature leader or mentor challenging, correcting, guiding, and trying to fulfill their duty to protect his brother. There is great flexibility when an individual carries out a ministry on his own, but there is often a more coordinated or regulated system when it involves the fellowship. It is a simple matter of organization and accountability.

> Obey your leaders and submit to them, for they keep watch over your souls as those who will give an account. Let them do this with joy and not with grief, for this would be unprofitable for you. — Heb. 13:17

Sometimes a person is getting "garbage" because he is missing something about himself or the process. Not everything is to be done in an individual way.

> From whom the whole body, being fitted and held together by what every joint supplies, according to the proper working of each individual part, causes the growth of the body for the building up of itself in love. — Eph. 4:16

The church should live at peace one with another and should be a place of encouragement.

> Finally, brethren, rejoice, be made complete, be comforted, be like-minded, live in peace; and the God of love and peace will be with you. — 2 Cor. 13:11

The church should provide exhortation and instruction and never be discouraging. It should be like-minded concerning beliefs and corporate direction from God, while celebrating the variety and beauty in the individual calling and gifting of God's children. Variety that comes from Him, and not from our selfish choices, creates strength in the body. Living in a church of discouragement and deconstruction instead of constructive teaching is a good reason to leave.

6. The Church Is Unjust to Other Members

There is nothing more painful than to watch a church being unjust and unfair to people. An unjust church that teaches or conducts themselves in unbiblical, self-serving ways is a good place to leave. It is horrible for any church to pressure, push, coerce, and take advantage of or use situational ethics with its people. Anger, frustration, and disgust burst from every decent person when an underdog gets oppressed and abused.

God is clear, neither leaders nor the followers are to be self-serving.

> And now, a word to you who are elders in the churches. I, too, am an elder and a witness to the sufferings of Christ. And I, too, will share his glory and his honor when he returns. As a fellow elder, this is my appeal to you: Care for the flock of God entrusted to you. Watch over it willingly, not grudgingly — not for what you will get out of it, but because you are eager to serve God. Don't lord it over the people assigned to your care, but lead them by your good example. And when the head Shepherd comes, your reward will be a never-ending share in his glory and honor. — 1 Pet. 5:1-4 (NLT)

Such oppressive injustice is most commonly characterized by the application of situational ethics. In regard to biblical doctrines and leadership, one answer should be good for all, and that one answer should be based upon a God-given, unchanging truth. People should be treated with respect as children of God. People should be taught consistently and fairly. People should be honored as God's selected ones. People should be held accountable only to God's standards and His ways. Only those that benefit or those that are caught in a cycle of abuse and ignorance want to belong to an unjust church.

Churches that teach submission as servanthood are unjust. Churches that teach that men should be dictators are unjust. Churches that miss the honor of women as equal servants of God and heirs to the throne are unjust. Churches that deny some opportunity because of class or status are unjust. Churches that are legalistic, saying, "Do this or you are not right before God" are unjust. This unfairness should nauseate the best and least of us.

Then Jesus spoke to the crowds and to His disciples, saying: "The scribes and the Pharisees have seated themselves in the chair of Moses; therefore all that they tell you, do and observe, but do not do according to their deeds; for they say things and do not do them. They tie up heavy burdens and lay them on men's shoulders, but they themselves are unwilling to move them with so much as a finger. But they do all their deeds to be noticed by men; for they broaden their phylacteries and lengthen the tassels of their garments. They love the place of honor at banquets and the chief seats in the synagogues, and respectful greetings in the market places, and being called Rabbi by men. But do not be called Rabbi; for One is your Teacher, and you are all brothers. Do not call anyone on earth your father; for One is your Father, He who is in heaven. Do not be called leaders; for One is your Leader, that is, Christ. But the greatest among you shall be your servant. Whoever exalts himself shall be humbled; and whoever humbles himself shall be exalted.

"But woe to you, scribes and Pharisees, hypocrites, because you shut off the kingdom of heaven from people; for you do not enter in yourselves, nor do you allow those who are entering to go in. [Woe to you, scribes and Pharisees, hypocrites, because you devour widows' houses, and for a pretense you make long prayers; therefore you will receive greater condemnation.]

"Woe to you, scribes and Pharisees, hypocrites, because you travel around on sea and land to make one proselyte; and when he becomes one, you make him twice as much a son of hell as yourselves.

"Woe to you, blind guides, who say, 'Whoever swears by the temple, that is nothing; but whoever swears by the gold of the temple is obligated.' You fools and blind men! Which is more important, the gold or the temple that sanctified the gold? And, 'Whoever swears by the altar, that is nothing, but whoever swears by the offering on it, he is obligated.' You blind men, which is more important, the offering, or the altar that sanctifies the offering?"— Matt. 23:1-19

We all love the films about the men and women who stand up for those treated unjustly. Even the fictitious martyrs like Braveheart are incredibly popular. We honor the heroes (often after the fact, or more specifically, after their death) who gave their lives to right the wrongs done to others.

There is no doubt that an injustice is a great reason to leave a church; however, before leaving, you need to ask: "If all of the heroes leave, who will rescue the damsel in distress? When will the injustice end?"

7. The Church Constantly Talks about Money

It is tiring when money, money, money is the talk of campaign after campaign in church after church. Sometime budgets are tight, sometime it seems that the people are cheap, and sometimes it seems like the leadership spends less than wisely. Who wants to go and worship God and hear a message on budgeting, tithing, and money? Who wants letter after letter about the financial status? Who wants to constantly be pushed to give more and more?

Constantly begging for money could be a good reason to change churches. Why should anyone want to go to a church that is materialistic or always trying to recover from bad decisions? The Bible clearly teaches that the church and every believer should plan well before heading out to do anything. Luke 14:28-30 reads,

> For which one of you, when he wants to build a tower, does not first sit down and calculate the cost to see if he has enough to complete it? Otherwise, when he has laid a foundation and is not able to finish, all who observe it begin to ridicule him, saying, "This man began to build and was not able to finish."

The primary lesson in this passage is that we are to follow God wisely. However, the application of this simple, very practical principle to church finances is easy: if a church is certain that God told them to do this or that financially, then the church should first ensure it can meet the need.

It is fair to get sick of hearing "give, give, give" and to question why so much time and teaching needs to be focused on that topic of money. It is fair to question the leadership and their wisdom when they "spend, spend, spend." It is fair to get tired of all the people who don't give and thus cause others to then constantly hear about giving.

Do we not have a right to be disgusted when hearing from the pulpit, "Well, the number one thing that Jesus talked about was money!" when in actuality, Jesus was talking about the same materialism coming from that comment. Do we not have a right to want to say to others in the church,

"Jesus also told His disciples to take nothing more than they needed and to go into ministry wasting neither money nor material things!"

Most leaders would love for someone who is sick and tired of hearing about money to stand up and say to the congregation, "Listen, I give. Why don't the rest of you obey God and give your best to God so that the ministry will go on? We need to focus on God and worship Him and not worry about the power bill." Most giving people would love to hear someone say, "Listen, I tithe and beyond. Why don't the leaders come up with a solution, even if the rest of the people are disobedient, that allows us to live within our means?"

Hearing about money all the time stinks. The pulpit is most definitely not designed for such discussions. Worship is not about money. Teaching about money all the time reveals much about the maturity of the leaders and the congregation. Hearing about money all the time might be a good reason to leave, but what if God is calling you to be that one who will stand up and challenge the church before leaving?

Even if you are not the one who should stand up, be quick to ask, "Did I vote for the budget that now requires all of this discussion?" If so, then your vote gave your word that you would support it financially regardless of circumstance. If the leadership is not following that plan, they should be challenged. If they are following the plan, the people who voted to support it should be challenged. Even if someone abstained, even if someone chose to let the leaders decide, that someone said "Yes" by their actions. Even if you are not the one to stand up and challenge the church, you should fulfill your commitment, because that commitment was to God and to His ministry—not to man. The Bible speaks of this commitment when it says, "Let your 'Yes' be 'Yes'" (Matt. 5:37).

8. The Church Is Run by a Dictatorship

The Bible shows the church is a collective of believers who are:

- all equal heirs to Christ.
- all given individual talents, capabilities, and abilities.
- all responsible for specific God-given tasks, duties, and authority.

A dictator is:

- a ruler with total power over a country, typically one who has obtained power by force.
- a person who tells people what to do in an autocratic way or who determines behavior in a particular sphere.
- (in ancient Rome) a chief magistrate with absolute power, appointed in an emergency.

If the church is run by a dictatorship or any other form of ungodly leadership, people have a good reason to leave. God is the only ruler over His church. Jesus is the only one who is able to judge the living and the dead in the world and in the church. No man, no person, and no set of people should try to execute total power or judgment outside of God's sphere or Word.

The definition of a dictator used the word autocratic. A summary of definitions from Dictionary.com gives an annotated definition of that word:

- of or relating to a ruler who has absolute power
- taking no account of other people's wishes or opinions; domineering

Clearly, no person is supposed to have absolute power. The God-ordained elder, pastor, or leader is but a servant anointed to guide, teach, and equip a local church. Even the apostles were only servants given authority over the churches they planted or served.

Most church members will quickly agree that any ungodly form of leadership, not just dictatorship, is a good reason to leave a church. However, do those followers ever ask their leaders to teach about biblical leadership style, structure, and authority? Do they check the leadership structure against their own Bible study? Though many leadership ideas are based on common sense, successful business or democratic ideals, these models cannot be biblically defended. Common sense and corporate business models are no substitute for God's clear instruction.

What is a biblical model of leadership? Does the Bible describe a system of servant-driven leadership? Does that model include the deacon-led church? Does it include regional bishops? Does the word deacon appear in the Bible as a leader? Is the pastor the leader?

Clearly, there is room for discussion and decision among the church—the people who are the heirs of the kingdom of God:

"Now look around among yourselves, brothers, and select seven men who are well respected and are full of the Holy Spirit and wisdom. We will put them in charge of this business. Then we can spend our time in prayer and preaching and teaching the word." This idea pleased the whole group, and they chose the following: Stephen (a man full of faith and the Holy Spirit), Philip, Procorus, Nicanor, Timon, Parmenas, and Nicolas of Antioch (a Gentile convert to the Jewish faith, who had now become a Christian). These seven were presented to the apostles, who

prayed for them as they laid their hands on them.—
Acts 6:3-6 (NLT)

While at the same time there is clear instruction to follow
the leaders:

Obey your leaders and submit to them, for they keep
watch over your souls as those who will give an
account. Let them do this with joy and not with grief,
for this would be unprofitable for you.—Heb. 13:17

As well, leaders should never be dictators:

Don't lord it over the people assigned to your care,
but lead them by your good example.—1 Pet. 5:3
(NLT)

An ungodly form of leadership is a good reason to leave
the church, but you need to be able to support any claim
of inappropriate leadership. You first must know what the
biblical defines as the proper leadership model. Search, study,
and respectfully ask the leaders for their biblical reasons.
Make sure that you address any concerns with their answers
before leaving. You may be the one who was "placed by God
in the unrighteous government for such a time of change as
this" (Esth. 4:14).

9. The Church Is Butting into My Family Life

People are indeed the masters of their own domain. God
has given every Christian some authority and responsibility
regarding their lives and the lives of their families. A husband
has the unique responsibility to lead his wife to God.

Husbands, love your wives, just as also Christ loved the church and gave Himself for her, to make her holy, cleansing her in the washing of water by the word. He did this to present the church to Himself in splendor, without spot or wrinkle or any such thing, but holy and blameless. — Eph. 5:25-27 (HCSB)

It is the husband and wife's job to lead any children to God.

These words that I am giving you today are to be in your heart. Repeat them to your children. Talk about them when you sit in your house and when you walk along the road, when you lie down and when you get up. — Deut. 6:6-7 (HCSB)

My son, observe the commandment of your father, and do not forsake the teaching of your mother; bind them continually on your heart; tie them around your neck. When you walk about, they will guide you; When you sleep, they will watch over you; And when you awake, they will talk to you. — Prov. 6:20-22

The children's job is to hold one another accountable to the leadership of their parents and to God's ways. Single adults are accountable for themselves. Businessmen are accountable for their businesses and have been given authority by God to lead that business.

Submit to every human institution because of the Lord, whether to the Emperor as the supreme authority, or to governors as those sent out by him to punish those who do evil and to praise those who do good. — 1 Pet. 2:13-14 (HCSB)

A church crossing its God-given boundaries of authority can be a good reason to leave. One denomination—actually, more like a cult—requires each member to have a mentor deacon that approves all work, family, dating, and financial decisions. One extreme example of overstepping God's boundaries is a church that requires a woman to have intercourse with her husband at his wish and intervenes publicly if she does not meet his needs. Another church requires a child to publicly confess private sin that has already been addressed by the parents, in order for the child to remain in church. The list goes on, to churches requiring the submission of tax forms for tithing verification and random drug testing of members.

Such flagrant and unloving intrusions are good reasons to leave. Moreover, though, there are far less obvious intrusions that overstep the church's bounds of authority and responsibility. The church is responsible for the corporate life and presentation of its members. The believers that make up the church have a God-given authority to maintain a pure and holy presentation of a holy God. Can the church accomplish its task without extending its authority beyond God's desire? Can the church keep the fellowship pure without violating the God-given authority that a person has over his own life? Where is the balance?

The fact that believers are given freedom of choice creates one limit of the church's authority. The church is no longer a "state-church," imprisoning people for personal sins. Each believer has the right to choose right or wrong. Believers can leave and end any authority that church was given over his life.

Likewise, the church has been given freedom of choice, and this freedom creates one limit of the individual's rights or authority. The Bible tells the church to separate from a person who sins publicly and won't change after loving challenges and discussion. The hope of the separation is that it will spur the person to repent (Matt 18:15-18). The church has the authority to separate from an unrighteous believer.

The story of Ananias in the book of Acts gives us another insight into God-given limits of authority:

> But a man named Ananias, with his wife Sapphira, sold a piece of property, and kept back some of the price for himself, with his wife's full knowledge, and bringing a portion of it, he laid it at the apostles' feet. But Peter said, "Ananias, why has Satan filled your heart to lie to the Holy Spirit and to keep back some of the price of the land? "While it remained unsold, did it not remain your own? And after it was sold, was it not under your control? Why is it that you have conceived this deed in your heart? You have not lied to men but to God." And as he heard these words, Ananias fell down and breathed his last; and great fear came over all who heard of it.—Acts 5:1-5

The questions, "While it remained unsold, did it not remain your own?" and "...after it was sold, was it not under your control?" illustrate that God had given the land to Ananias; it was his to manage. The church had no rights over the land and had no right to tell Ananias what to do with it. This biblical teaching is consistent with other Bible instructions to "give as we see fit in our hearts" and to "serve God willingly and not under compulsion" and for elders to "not rule over or force the people."

Ultimately the church is to serve, worship, learn, and minister with one another and see God change the lives of each person. The church must protect the name and testimony of Christ, but at the same time, its local authority is limited to the corporate life of the believers and those actions or issues that affect the corporate life of believers. The church is not to create laws or judge the heart of a man.

A church that exceeds its biblically defined reach is a good church to leave. Before you leave, though, make sure you aren't simply trying to live life your own way. There is no living life one's own way for Christians. Believers are given authority over their lives, but Christians have submitted their authority to Christ and must live in a biblical way. There is no escape from that commitment, and when the church challenges believers to live to their commitment, it is not butting into personal lives but rather exercising the very clear responsibility of the church.

10. The Church is Impersonal

While some people are troubled by the church being too involved in their lives, others are troubled by the church not being personal enough. Thousands and thousands of people leave from large churches every year because they need friends and closeness. Other people are flocking to the large church to be one in a crowd. There are mature and immature believers in both of these types of people.

The biblical description of a church definitely reflects a personal, close fellowship—a family—living together while sharing everything. The church died together, standing bold and testifying, in the Roman arenas. There was no question about the need for identity, accountability, and closeness. The New Testament church reflected a movement of thousands with identity and fraternity of the believers. Everyone has the right to a personal church.

> Then he left there and went to the house of a man named Titius Justus, a worshiper of God, whose house was next to the synagogue.—Acts 18:7

> And all those who had believed were together and had all things in common; and they began selling

their property and possessions and were sharing them with all, as anyone might have need. Day by day continuing with one mind in the temple, and breaking bread from house to house, they were taking their meals together with gladness and sincerity of heart, praising God and having favor with all the people. And the Lord was adding to their number day by day those who were being saved. — Acts 2:44-47

Whether a church is impersonal or personal is not directly related to how many friends or small groups there are in the church. Impersonality takes other forms too:

- The "Fake Preacher Voice": words spoken and taught with unreal emphasis and tone solely for the sake of oration are impersonal at best.
- Stolen sermons, other men's words, and passions lacking the personal preparation or passion of the teacher that aren't even personal to the teacher.
- State-of-the-art productions, where the end goal is not the effective presentation of biblical truth but the entertainment of consumers, is distant and focused on itself.
- "Blah, blah" classes, those taught because they should be by less inspired teachers, are truly impersonal." Let's do lunch" leader and members, the ones promising interaction without even an intention of making time, aren't even personally personal.
- Church inattentiveness to the needs of the believers is the result of corporate impersonality.

Who would want to remain bound to such a façade? Personal is not about marketing, direct contact, or timely emails. Personal is about how many deep, binding brother and sister relationships a person experiences. Personal is about people, real people, touching the lives of real people. Personal is knowing other people. Personal involves people.

Impersonality in church life could be a good reason to change churches, but it might be interesting to ask:

- How did I get involved in an impersonal church?
- Was it this way when I came here?
- Have I simply grown to a point where I am ready for discipleship involving accountability?
- Have I matured to a point where I need people?
- Did the church become impersonal, or did I need impersonal when I came here?

You should answer these questions before leaving. There is always a possibility that your new awareness should be taught by you at your impersonal church. If, and only if, God approves of the move to more intimacy can impersonality be a good reason to leave.

A Good Reason to Leave Is Often a Reason to Stay

Leaders and followers need to remember this: leaving is not the problem; it is the way people leave that is the problem. A person can leave well, and God can be glorified when His will is accomplished. There are good reasons to leave, but sometimes a good reason to leave is an excellent reason to stay. In every one of the ten good reasons to leave discussed above, there was always a reason to stay. Sometimes the reason was to fight for justice, to hold high the truth of God, or to help abolish the dictatorship. In other cases, the reason to stay was so that the final "living" person would not take the last "life" from the church or that the name of Jesus Christ would not die a hypocritical death in the community.

Unfortunately, when a good reason to leave becomes God's reason for you to stay, life can be difficult. Friends already on the exit do not understand why you are staying. Some of those staying wish you would leave. If God leads you to stay, you will often become like a prophet, teacher, or thorn that reminds a church of righteousness. If this is your call, be gracious, friendly, and full of goodness as you stay. Stay with a God-given purpose of revival or silent prayer. Here's one man's true story:

> I will never forget being in my office worrying over my role as associate pastor/youth guy/singles leader while watching my world crumble as I lived (as a staff member) through a church split. I was devastated, disgusted, tired, and I couldn't figure out who was right. Each side—all twelve of them—had good points and bad points.

In the beginning, I kept trying to figure out what side I was on. I could never find peace because I was young, because both sides were friends, because I had up to that point been involved in the best church ever, and because I didn't like the split. One family would try to pull me this way and another family would try to pull me that way. A person would vent about one thing and another would vent about the other side. Every discussion was about the trial, and every discussion focused on "over-talking" this horrible event. Everyone had an opinion, and I was quickly getting a battlefield promotion as leaders left.

I couldn't take it any longer. I cried out to God. It was then, that God led me to a Scripture that changed my life:

> "For lack of wood the fire goes out, and where there is no whisperer, contention quiets down. Like charcoal to hot embers and wood to fire, so is a conten-

tious man to kindle strife. The words of a whisperer are like dainty morsels, and they go down into the innermost parts of the body. Like an earthen vessel overlaid with silver dross are burning lips and a wicked heart. He who hates disguises it with his lips, but he lays up deceit in his heart. When he speaks graciously, do not believe him, for there are seven abominations in his heart. Though his hatred covers itself with guile, his wickedness will be revealed before the assembly. He who digs a pit will fall into it, and he who rolls a stone, it will come back on him. A lying tongue hates those it crushes, and a flattering mouth works ruin."—Prov. 26:20-28

And then came my answer from God: Stay.

"Stay?" I asked. "Stay why? Who is right? What do I do?'

"Stay," the Spirit confirmed in my heart.

"But who...what...?"

"You asked what you should do; take no sides and stay, because I called you here. Do not involve yourself in the struggle except to promote righteousness in choices and discussions. I call you to stay."

This is the best that I can word what I knew in my heart that day. God told me to stay. How incredible! I had my answer. God even told me He would protect me, and those who deceived would get theirs. He told me not to be happy but to mourn for them. He showed me that in the end, He would show right from wrong. He showed me that the end might be in heaven. He told me to stay. I wrote the scripture on a poster board, and to this day it hangs in my office.

The weirdest thing happened as I began to share God's clear, biblical, and personal answer to me ("stay"). People got mean, mad, and didn't want to hear my answer. As people would start the discussions, I would try to get away or divert them. When pushed to render an opinion, I would say, "I don't know what is right or wrong. God has not told me what the church should do, what anyone should do, or who is right or wrong. All He has told me is that I am to stay. So I am going to stay." I was excited because I had this great simple answer from God—stay. The more I disengaged from all the "split stuff" the more some people got mad. Many friends were no longer friends, and my popularity waned with others. There was a remnant who heard from God in the same way, but even we could not console one another as the church split apart.

The years progressed, and I realized that spiritually imma-ture people should never start a church and that every church needs a great covering of wise mentors. There were no old guys, no experienced guys to show us the signs of disaster that were looming on the horizon. Our common enemy had a field day and won a battle. I realized that the people who got frustrated with me when I would not take sides did so because they were convicted. They had no answer, were confused, and could not stand that someone had an answer. It drove them nuts that someone would no longer join the fray.

It wasn't easy, but I stayed. Others stayed as well, while both good and bad people left as casualties of war. It was not easy, but it was right. A good reason to leave had become a great reason to stay. The name of Christ did not die in that community, and to this day that church is one of the most clear, solid, and steady lights of Christ in its community.

It is very simple. A good reason cannot be acted on when it becomes a great reason to stay. The church needs more people who will stay for revival. The church is a disaster and full of all kinds of ills rising from secular schemes, weak doctrine, and wrong motives. We may need to ask God if He wants us to help stop the leaks before everyone simply abandons the ship. Even better, it might not be such a bad idea for us to make sure we did not help engineer the leaks.

What would happen if people stayed, stood for righteousness, and became engineers of a solution instead of giving up and seeking a place that was better for them? Each person must make certain that his good reason to leave has become the one great reason to leave before he changes churches.

Chapter 3

Ten Poor Reasons to Leave

A key piece of knowledge on the subject of leaving a church is this:

There are poor reasons to leave a church.

Once again, both leaders and followers need to remember, the issue is not leaving but leaving well. The goal is for people to leave well and to glorify God in their departure. People are people of choice. They can leave well, or they can leave poorly.

People who leave well:

- Share a similar life, philosophy, and approach.
- Always leave for a good reason.
- Leave for one great reason regardless of their specific good reason.

People leaving poorly:

- Share a similar life, philosophy, and approach.
- Always leave for a bad reason.
- Leave for one terrible reason, regardless of their specific bad reason.

- Generally, do not even realize that they are leaving poorly.

When a person leaves well, he is given credit for his decision and is honored. The time has come for the church to begin to fearlessly giving credit to the person who leaves poorly and hold him accountable for his decision. How much does the church love the believer who is planning or executing a poor departure? Do they care that he may not know the personal consequences that come from a poor departure? Does the church care enough to challenge the believer and ask: "If you were to be crucified, your life taken, your honor stripped from you, and hung on a cross for this decision—are you sure that you would die for it? Are you so sure that this is what God wants that you would die for it?"

Christians must be willing to look into the why, how, and what of leaving poorly if they want to keep people from regretting such a decision. The church cannot chastise or scorn one who departs poorly without being convicted of a crime before God. God's Word will reveal to them very simply:

> Brothers, even if anyone is caught in any trespass, you who are spiritual, restore such a one in a spirit of gentleness; each one looking to yourself, so that you too will not be tempted. —Gal. 6:1

The beginning of this look into the workings of a poor departure begins with the many common statements made by those that have, or wish they had already, departed. Statements like these are quoted by people justifying their departures:

- My kids do not like the church.
- My teens just are not getting involved.

- Worship just does not do it for me.
- I just cannot get over_____.
- I think we are going a separate way.
- Things have just changed.
- I am not comfortable anymore.
- I am not being allowed to serve.
- The worship is so much better at_____.
- There are so many kids at_____.
- The preaching is so great at_____.
- I am not sure we agree with everything here.
- I do not agree with the direction of the church.

The follower senses something wrong with the answer even though it seems to make sense. The long-term leader holds his tongue because he has heard these statements repeatedly through the years. A wise person quickly realizes that, among the many weaknesses of these statements, selfishness and idealism reign supreme. All of the reasons given are about what "I, me, or we" want or need. The unspoken words reflect a complaint about what "they, them, he, or she" aren't providing.

But is it not fair to expect your needs to be met by the church? Isn't that what church is all about? Is it not fair to expect a local church to be consistent with the Bible in its approach, ministry, and teaching? Isn't it fair to expect the leaders to be holy and sold out to God as they unselfishly lead? The Bible teaches that believers are to help other believers and meet their needs. There is no question that the church should be providing quality, biblically consistent ministry to believers.

Carry one another's burdens; in this way you will fulfill the law of Christ. — Gal. 6:2 (HCSB)

> If anyone has this world's goods and sees his brother in need but shuts off his compassion from him—how can God's love reside in him? —1 John 3:17 (HCSB)

However, we also must realize that every believer is a part of the church he attends. If his church does not have a good youth program and he is not helping out, then he is as much a part of the problem as any other person is, because he is the church. If the teaching is not all it can be, and he has not become a scholar or is not teaching, then he is part of the problem. If he is not at peace but he does not have a better, biblically based idea or teaching, then he is as much the problem as the rest of the church. Simply put, if you say, "They aren't..." in the context of church, you are admitting that you are part of the problem. If people leave based on "they" statements, people leave poorly.

The church is not supposed to be a consumer relationship where the member comes to get what he needs. Nor is the church to be an entirely servant relationship where the member comes only to give. Someone once said of marriage, "Marriage is not 50-50 but instead both the husband and wife giving 100 percent of themselves."

No truer statement could be made of the church member and the rest of his church. Both partners are to serve the other before themselves. If they both serve, they both receive. Jesus Christ described His church as a fellowship, a family, a partnership, and a body.

Church is family. Church is about what the fellowship has. If the fellowship doesn't have food, then the leaders and members should do everything they can to help the church get food. If the church needs a stronger youth ministry, everyone gives more, helps more, prays more, and offers to do whatever they can to serve the family so that the family can have a better youth ministry. If the church needs different worship styles, everyone prays, seeks, learns, and makes a good biblical argument so that the family can have everything that God would want them to have.

Unfortunately, people often see themselves as consumers who come to get. They do not see themselves as family, partners, warriors, and friends who do everything possible to get the body what it needs. Consumerism is one of the central philosophies of those who leave poorly—and, often, they do not even know it.

The increasingly transient and disposable cultures of North America and Europe can easily be observed. An individual making a lifelong commitment to other believers in the church is almost unthinkable in a world where people quickly discard husbands, wives, and the elderly when it is no longer desirable or convenient to live through the challenges of family. Commitment to the greater cause stands little chance of survival in the face of graduates and workers who believe they are entitled to be paid and expect companies to be thankful they showed up to work. Selflessness is unlikely in churches full of people who truly believe that they have a God-given right to vote based on their opinion. A society that turns away from the study of history while turning to TV personalities peddling their advice for money and success stands little chance of seeing the beauty of committing to long-term truth.

These societal shifts seem to cry out, "If you do not like it, leave it. If you like it, you need it—get it now. If it does not fit, you change it. If you cannot change it, discard it. If you want more, get it. Now! Now! Now!" Capitalism has become equivalent with greed. Instant self-gratification has become a piece of our culture. Adults no longer know the beauty of a well-seasoned desire being fulfilled through patience, hard work, and legitimacy. People who would never have filed bankruptcy for the shame of failure bankrupt their fellow believers at church and move on to an easier life.

Departing poorly is a self-centered and transient choice that seeks only to meet personal needs. Diagnosing the problem does little but raise awareness for people, who, if they are truly leaving poorly, are most likely going to deny the diagnosis anyway. However, diagnosis of poor departures can provide a preventative, protective measure for people who have not even thought about leaving. As reviewing "Ten Good Reasons to Leave" proved healthy, exploring "Ten Poor Reasons to Leave" is healthy medicine for avoiding leaving poorly. Looking at these reasons also will help us live a great corporate life at church even if we are not leaving.

1. My Kids Do Not Like It Here or Are Not Getting Involved

Church is great when it is a blast. Churches should strive to teach children in interesting and relevant ways. Parents hate dragging their kids to anything, especially something seen as optional. Life with and disciplining children is difficult enough without feeling like you have to drag your kids to church.

However, this reason is a poor reason to leave, because it makes four critical assumptions about church, kids, and parents:

- Church is optional.
- All aspects of church should be fun for kids.
- The kids hear from God more clearly than parents do.
- The parents want to go to church.

Is church optional? No. The answer for the believer is clear. God has commanded believers to rear their children among the fellowship that they are part of:

And let us not neglect our meeting together, as some people do, but encourage and warn each other, especially now that the day of his coming back again is drawing near. — Heb. 10:25 (NLT)

If church is not optional, then how about fun? Shouldn't church be fun for children? Kids do not always like school, but parents and teachers wish they would. Kids do not always like vegetables, but they need them. Kids do not like going to bed, but they need sleep. Children do not like many things that parents require for the child's best interest. Could it be that children don't like church because they are wrong? Could it be that the kids might like church if parents got involved, got them involved, and simply said, "Have fun." How many children would choose to go to school on their own? But because of the expectation that attendance is mandatory, the children go.

There is no way any church can provide fun everything for every child all of the time, especially if the church intends on teaching — really teaching. The biblical call is for children to learn about God — to mature. Their primary teachers should be their parents. The God-called teachers at church should complement and build up the parents' biblical instruction.

Fathers, do not provoke your children to anger, but bring them up in the discipline and instruction of the Lord. — Eph. 6:4

And you must commit yourselves wholeheartedly to these commands I am giving you today. Repeat them again and again to your children. Talk about them when you are at home and when you are away on a journey, when you are lying down and when you are getting up again. — Deut. 6:6-7 (NLT)

The church needs to be sensitive when parents say, "My children do not have any friends here." Every parent wants their child to have friends at church. However, children who would never choose to go to school every day seem to make plenty of friends when parents simply take them and require them to attend. Their friendships are a result of consistent geographic location. Children will find friends at church if parents simply bring them regularly and involve their family in the life of the church.

Parents need to remember that they are the leaders of the children. If a child is not going to choose to learn at the current church, what is the likelihood that he will choose to learn at the next church? Do children choose the family's house or their parents' jobs? Even more important, what is a parent teaching a child when the family changes churches because the child does not like the program? Would parents let children make life-changing investment decisions when the children do not even understand compound interest, much less the idea of retirement?

Youth ministers know the most important things a parent can do to get their teen involved are to make time in the teen's schedules, bring their teens, and encourage their teens. Are parents good role models? If not, the teen will not stay involved anywhere the parent goes, because the parent will not have the stamina to support him. New locations do not produce new commitments.

The worst assumption this argument makes is that parents really want to be at any church, much less a challenging, teaching church. This poor reason to leave is often only an excuse for parents who do not want to get involved or who want to find something different.

The church and the parents need to clearly understand that church for children is not a game but a time of preparation and teaching of God's truths that can change their lives and protect them in the future. The bottom line is that learning the Bible and applying truth is more about survival than fun. However, church can be fun if the parents get involved and help lead the church.

2. Worship Just Does Not Do It for Me

On the surface, this poor reason for leaving seems to have merit. Shouldn't people enjoy worship? Shouldn't believers have the right to really get into worship and hear great teaching? Shouldn't the gathering of believers be incredible? Though the answer to all of these questions is yes, this line of thinking is entirely focused on the believer and not on God. This thinking assumes:

- Worship is for the believer and should appeal to the believer.
- Good worship always returns a felt benefit for the worshipper.
- Corporate, or group, worship is the beginning of personal worship.

Is worship for the believer? Should worship services be designed to appeal to the believer or to God? Here is an important truth to Christianity: worship isn't for people. America has become a people who say they are worshipping God but who are really just getting an emotional or spiritual fix. Don't be mistaken—a byproduct of worship is personal renewal, but worship is not for you. Worship is always pointed at the object worshipped. If a person worships only to get something from that which is worshipped, he borders on practicing idolatry. Christian worship is for God because He is God. Worship is a response to seeing God, to being aware of Him, and to being overwhelmed by His awesomeness. Christian worship is man's response to a holy God.

> All the sons of Israel, seeing the fire come down and
> the glory of the LORD upon the house, bowed down
> on the pavement with their faces to the ground, and
> they worshiped and gave praise to the LORD, saying,
> "Truly He is good, truly His lovingkindness is ever-
> lasting."—2 Chron. 7:3

Worship services would not require much design if the
goal is to reveal the God we stand in awe of, to honor the
God that the church already worships, and to raise a collective voice in prayer, praise, and adoration.

Does good worship always result in a return on investment for the worshipper? Worship is giving, not taking, but
there has never been a person who offered their best to God
and did not walk away changed. Regardless of the style,
professionalism, or words of a particular worship service,
people who sing to God, pray to Him, and worship Him will
be blessed. The Bible teaches:

> But You are holy, O You Who dwell in the praises of
> Israel.—Ps. 22:3 (AMP)

On the other hand, the motive of worship is destroyed
when a believer goes to worship to get something in return.
Group worship is about gathering together to stand in awe
because of what His Spirit has already revealed inside of us.
Jesus taught, "But an hour is coming, and now is, when the
true worshipers will worship the Father in spirit and truth;
for such people the Father seeks to be His worshipers" (John
4:23).

The statement "Worship just doesn't do it for me" reveals
that a person doesn't understand worship and is not worshipping God. When he does find a worship service that does
it for him, it will probably be the worldly part of the new
service that excites him. In true worship, people no longer

say, "The band is incredible!" or "The teacher is great!" Instead they proclaim, "God is here!"

Worship expects nothing in return, though true worship is always rewarded. It was this way in the beginning and it will be this way in the end.

And He came and took the book out of the right hand of Him who sat on the throne. When He had taken the book, the four living creatures and the twenty-four elders fell down before the Lamb, each one holding a harp and golden bowls full of incense, which are the prayers of the saints. And they sang a new song, saying, "Worthy are You to take the book and to break its seals; for You were slain, and purchased for God with Your blood men from every tribe and tongue and people and nation. "You have made them to be a kingdom and priests to our God; and they will reign upon the earth."

Then I looked, and I heard the voice of many angels around the throne and the living creatures and the elders; and the number of them was myriads of myriads, and thousands of thousands, saying with a loud voice, "Worthy is the Lamb that was slain to receive power and riches and wisdom and might and honor and glory and blessing." And every created thing which is in heaven and on the earth and under the earth and on the sea, and all things in them, I heard saying, "To Him who sits on the throne, and to the Lamb, be blessing and honor and glory and dominion forever and ever." And the four living creatures kept saying, "Amen." And the elders fell down and worshiped."—Rev. 5:7-14

3. I Think We Are Going a Separate Way

It is okay for people to desire different ministries and to be called to different works in various places. The Church is broader than any local church. The Church is the sum of all believing Christians everywhere. Christians live in a unified diversity as they serve one God, with one goal in many places and in many ways. They are unified by one God, by one Faith, by one way to the Father:

> There is one body and one Spirit, just as also you were called in one hope of your calling; one Lord, one faith, one baptism, one God and Father of all who is over all and through all and in all.
> But to each one of us grace was given according to the measure of Christ's gift. Therefore it says, "WHEN HE ASCENDED ON HIGH, HE LED CAPTIVE A HOST OF CAPTIVES, AND HE GAVE GIFTS TO MEN."—Eph. 4:4-8

> Jesus said to him, "I am the way, and the truth, and the life; no one comes to the Father but through Me."—John 14:6

And, by one single purpose from Christ's first arrival until He comes again:

> You are the salt of the earth. But what good is salt if it has lost its flavor? Can you make it useful again? It will be thrown out and trampled underfoot as worthless. You are the light of the world—like a city on a mountain, glowing in the night for all to see. Don't hide your light under a basket! Instead, put it on a stand and let it shine for all. In the same way, let your good deeds shine out for all to see, so that everyone will praise your heavenly Father.—Matt. 5:13-16 NLT

> He who loves his life loses it, and he who hates his life in this world will keep it to life eternal. If anyone serves Me, he must follow Me; and where I am, there

My servant will be also; if anyone serves Me, the Father will honor him. —John 12:25-26

Jesus' followers were all desperate people needing forgiveness and grace so they could be restored to a great relationship with their Father in heaven. Jesus is that way, and the Spirit is the guide to the journey. Many Christians fail to realize all Christians are still desperate people in need of the Spirit to guide them. Christians are totally dependent on the work of Jesus to enter into rest and needing wisdom from the Father. They are all still desperate people who cannot stand on their own. They need God.

Christians are also unified in purpose. They are to continue to follow God and while following Him, bring glory to His Name. This type of living is a total sacrifice of our life on earth to serve Him. We are unified by following Him, living His truths, and being 100 percent available at any moment for His service, whether in worship or to another.

How can anyone not see the majesty of how a tree comes from a small seed with some cells being engineered to turn into bark and others to pulp and others branching out? Human life should bring the same awe of God's beauty, creativity, and variety in His creation. Christians are very different people even though they are unified in Spirit, purpose, and belief. God teaches that this diversity is their strength, as many different parts come together and create the whole. The church is made up of all kinds of people, talents, and gifts. People will serve God in varying ways. Some will go, and others will send. Some will teach, and others will preach. He will lead people to serve Him in different ways, but when all the variety comes together, we will be complete. The church, your local church, is supposed to be diverse and yet entirely unified. This unified diversity means that sometimes we will do different things, in different ways, with different callings, in different places. However, when people say, "I think we are going our separate ways," they are not usually implying or living unity. There are some very common, poor assumptions that are made when people leave for this reason:

- "Going our separate ways" implies unified diversity.
- Reconciliation of ideas is not required as long as people say, "Everything is okay."
- Agreeing to disagree is biblical and fixes everything.

Does the statement "going our separate ways" imply unified diversity? Not usually. More often "going our separate ways" is a vague feeling or comment made to cover up, to avoid, or to ensure a peaceful departure. People feel better saying, "We are just headed different ways," but everyone knows what the statement means. The statement is as lame as breaking up, saying, "Let's just be friends." If God is really drawing a believer to a new work, wouldn't the believer be excited to share the idea and have his family confirm it instead of sneaking or slipping out the back? If you feel this way, you need to ask, "What way are they going, and what different way am I going?" People need to be unified and to love one another before they depart. If the departure is of God, the church needs to have a great sending off with anointing, blessing, prayer, and praise. Departing to a new place—even when different—can be an incredibly unifying event when it is celebrated of God. "Going our separate ways" will never reach the high goal of unified diversity.

Can people avoid reconciling ideas as long as they say, "Everything is okay"? Interestingly, God wants His people to be of the same mind, and that requires peaceful reconciliation of ideas not just actions.

Therefore if there is any encouragement in Christ, if there is any consolation of love, if there is any fellowship of the Spirit, if any affection and compas-

sion, make my joy complete by being of the same
mind, maintaining the same love, united in spirit,
intent on one purpose. Do nothing from selfishness
or empty conceit, but with humility of mind regard
one another as more important than yourselves; do
not merely look out for your own personal interests,
but also for the interests of others. — Phil. 2:1-4

Reconciliation is not the process of solving problems.
Reconciliation is the process of discovering why two things
that should be the same are not the same. Growing believers
may not always believe the same thing, understand a scripture the same way, or initially hear the same thing from God.
Surely, unity will come with enough prayer, study and maturity; however, it is unacceptable for believers to not be at
peace with one another. It is not acceptable to be divided in
spirit! There is only one God and one truth, so in any one
situation, there can be only one God answer. This simple
logic is demonstrated again and again throughout God's
history as He requires all men to adhere to the same principles in varying circumstances.

For example, the Antioch Gentiles (non-Jewish
Christians) were told by Jewish Christians that they needed
to be circumcised and follow all of the Old Testament laws
in order to be acceptable to God. This debate was so huge
and the believers were having trouble believing the leaders
of their church. Did the church at Antioch just go their separate way? Did the apostles say, "Well, these Jewish Christian
teachers just need to go their way, and we will go our way?"
No. The church leaders understood that unity, more than
anything else, was the single thing Jesus brings to mankind.
They understood there is one Spirit and there is one answer
for all who would walk in truth. The church leaders gathered together, discussed, prayed, and sought God. As they
discussed, the leaders presented this:

"God, who knows people's hearts, confirmed that he accepts Gentiles by giving them the Holy Spirit, just as he gave him to us. He made no distinction between us and them, for he also cleansed their hearts through faith. Why are you now questioning God's way by burdening the Gentile believers with a yoke that neither we nor our ancestors were able to bear? We believe that we are all saved the same way, by the special favor of the Lord Jesus."

There was no further discussion, and everyone listened as Barnabas and Paul told about the miraculous signs and wonders God had done through them among the Gentiles.

When they had finished, James stood and said, "Brothers, listen to me. Peter has told you about the time God first visited the Gentiles to take from them a people for himself. And this conversion of Gentiles agrees with what the prophets predicted. For instance, it is written: 'Afterward I will return, and I will restore the fallen kingdom of David. From the ruins I will rebuild it, and I will restore it, so that the rest of humanity might find the Lord, including the Gentiles—all those I have called to be mine. This is what the Lord says, he who made these things known long ago.'

And so my judgment is that we should stop troubling the Gentiles who turn to God, except that we should write to them and tell them to abstain from eating meat sacrificed to idols, from sexual immorality, and from consuming blood or eating the meat of strangled animals. For these laws of Moses have been preached in Jewish synagogues in every city on every Sabbath for many generations.".—Acts 15:7-21 (NLT)

The Holy Spirit led the apostles and church through a long and tiring issue using truth, the Old Testament, and Jesus' teachings to reach one single conclusion. That conclusion was documented in a letter sent to Antioch:

> Then the apostles and elders and the whole church in Jerusalem chose delegates, and they sent them to Antioch of Syria with Paul and Barnabas to report on this decision. The men chosen were two of the church leaders—Judas (also called Barsabbas) and Silas. This is the letter they took along with them:

> "This letter is from the apostles and elders, your brothers in Jerusalem. It is written to the Gentile believers in Antioch, Syria, and Cilicia. Greetings!

> "We understand that some men from here have troubled you and upset you with their teaching, but they had no such instructions from us.

> So it seemed good to us, having unanimously agreed on our decision, to send you these official representatives, along with our beloved Barnabas and Paul, who have risked their lives for the sake of our Lord Jesus Christ.

> So we are sending Judas and Silas to tell you what we have decided concerning your question. "For it seemed good to the Holy Spirit and to us to lay no greater burden on you than these requirements:

> You must abstain from eating food offered to idols, from consuming blood or eating the meat of strangled animals, and from sexual immorality. If you do this, you will do well. Farewell."

The four messengers went at once to Antioch, where they called a general meeting of the Christians and delivered the letter. And there was great joy throughout the church that day as they read this encouraging message. — Acts 15:22-31 (NLT)

Christians will face potentially dividing issues. Believers will face uncomfortable circumstances together. People generally try to avoid conflict and pursue simple solutions. However, being separated in Spirit or Truth cannot be acceptable to any true leader or follower.

Does agreeing to disagree fix everything simply because people agree? People leaving because "we are going separate ways" often quote the scripture about Paul and Barnabas when the two missionaries could not agree on a crew. They say, "Well, look at Paul and Barnabas. They could not decide who to take on their missionary journey, and both of them were godly. In the end, they still could not agree, so they decided to go their separate ways in ministry." The biblical account, however, tells an entirely different story in its words, spirit, and implication.

After some time Paul said to Barnabas, "Let's return to each city where we previously preached the word of the Lord, to see how the new believers are getting along." Barnabas agreed and wanted to take along John Mark. But Paul disagreed strongly, since John Mark had deserted them in Pamphylia and had not shared in their work. Their disagreement over this was so sharp that they separated. Barnabas took John Mark with him and sailed for Cyprus. Paul chose Silas, and the believers sent them off, entrusting them to the Lord's grace. — Acts 15:36-40 (NLT)

An objective reading does not indicate that this disagreement was godly or positive. In fact, the phrase "it was so sharp" combined with the passion and zeal of Paul indicates anything but a positive experience.

To use this historical record to defend the practice of "going our separate ways" requires the reader to read into the text while ignoring clear biblical truths. With regard to reading into the text, this historical record only records the decisions as history without telling the reader whether the decisions were good or bad. To assume that anything beyond the fact that Paul and Barnabas disagreed sharply is irresponsible. Historical record cannot always be used to make absolute truths to live by. For example, how ridiculous would it be for someone to argue, "I am terrified, surrounded by my enemies, I feel oppressed. I am going to end my life. After all, Saul took his life in the Bible when he was surrounded by those who sought to destroy him"? Regardless of Saul's history, the Bible is clear that taking anyone's life is wrong. In the same way, just because Paul and Barnabas split up, does not mean that the church should. Just because this was their choice does not mean it was right. Not even Paul claimed to be without error.

With regard to examining other biblical truths, the Bible is abundantly clear that believers can and should get along, live in peace, and be unified. When God calls unified and peaceful people to new ministries, the phrase "going our separate ways" will never be used.

4. Things Have Just Changed

Many people really dislike change. Constant change can be an indicator of instability. Constant change creates an overwhelming feeling that causes people to often ask, "Why do we have to change all the time? Do we know what we are doing?" Too much change can result in an uncomfortable ministry style or method. On the other hand, not all change is bad. Sometimes people claiming "things have just changed" make some poor assumptions when using this reason to leave:

- The perception of change is the reality of change.
- The church has changed.
- Different is bad.
- Too much change is not good.

Does feeling that things have changed mean things have changed? Is a personal perception of change objective proof of change? Not really. Human feelings and emotions—even for believers—can often swing high and low, left and right. In times of stress, busyness, a lack of time with God, and being disconnected from other believers, people can find themselves feeling all kinds of things that are untrustworthy. If you are feeling like you want to leave because "things have changed," get a pen and paper and ask, "What is it, factually, that has changed?" You may find that you cannot make a very long list. You may also be challenged when some of the changes seem consistent with biblical teaching.

Has the church changed? Many people leaving because they feel like "the church has changed" fail to include on their list of changes things that have changed about their lives. Do you go to church as much? Are you still involved in serving? Are you studying daily? Do you hang out with the people from church? Is the church fellowship a priority? All of these are interesting questions, but even more interesting are the non-church questions. Did someone die in your family? Did you just get married? Has your financial picture changed? Have you made a grave error? Personal change brings a change in perspective and, often, a different view of life. Many times the people have changed far more than the church that has changed.

Is everything different bad? Two questions open up this thought process: "Is there any area of your life in which you have not experienced change?" and "What did you do when you experienced change in other areas?" When your marriage changed, did you separate? When your kids hit puberty, did you leave? When the hours changed at work, did you quit? Not all change is bad, even when it is a difficult change. Puberty is a huge, difficult, physical change, but thank God we get to mature into adults! Spiritual changes will mimic this physical change. Some job changes and policy changes are difficult but result in tremendous efficiency and improvement in quality of life. Any change consistent with the Bible and led of God will always result in good. If the new thing at church is really a problem, it will be easy to state, factually, what the problem is instead of saying vaguely, "things have just changed." If there is not an apparent problem or, more importantly, a biblical problem, then perhaps the change is being used by God. What if God wants the change to change the people? What if God wants to change you?

The person who leaves a church because of change might find himself doomed to continually go from church to church. After all, change is guaranteed. The mature believer needs to be filled with the Spirit of God and learn to not only endure but also to succeed through the changes of life. Paul stated this perfectly in Philippians:

> Not that I am referring to being in need; for I have learned to be content with whatever I have. I know what it is to have little, and I know what it is to have plenty. In any and all circumstances I have learned the secret of being well-fed and of going hungry, of having plenty and of being in need. I can do all things through him who strengthens me. — Phil. 4:11-13 (NRSV)

Is too much change bad? Jesus came and turned the world upside down. He issued forth change by changing people's motives from serving the law to serving God. The Pharisees (the "church" leaders of those days) were criticized by Jesus for holding on to their own traditions and ignoring His teaching.

> So the Pharisees and teachers of religious law asked him, "Why don't your disciples follow our age-old customs? For they eat without first performing the hand-washing ceremony."
> Jesus replied, "You hypocrites! Isaiah was prophesying about you when he said, 'These people honor me with their lips, but their hearts are far away. Their worship is a farce, for they replace God's commands with their own man-made teachings.' For you ignore God's specific laws and substitute your own traditions." Then he said, "You reject God's laws in order to hold on to your own traditions."—Mark 7:5-9 (NLT)

Even though change occurs, some things should not change. God does not change, and what He teaches us to do should not change. If people are convinced of Him, they should follow His teaching without trying to change it. Paul wrote just this point to the new believers in Jesus:

> So then, brethren, stand firm and hold to the traditions which you were taught, whether by word of mouth or by letter from us.—2 Thess. 2:15

You need to be willing to change when the Bible or the Spirit of God initiates the change, and you need to be unwilling to change what the Bible or the Spirit of God makes absolutely clear to us. Change is going to occur. If there is a biblical, Christian problem with a change, it should be addressed. Otherwise, people need to be careful not to leave for such a poor reason.

5. I Do Not Feel Like Part of the Family Anymore

There have always been churches that do not embrace or champion connections among the people. There have been people who go to church out of obedience with no desire for fellowship. There are people who have no desire to experience the accountability and transparency of feeling like family. However, anyone who has experienced the healthy, happy feeling of being family with a church will never want to go back to distance and simple attendance. The person who has tasted the beauty of transparency and connection of true fellowship will never be able to be satisfied if he finds himself disconnected from fellowship, friends, or family.

One perception of change can be feeling as if you are no longer part of the family. This, however, is a poor reason, based solely on feeling. There are three assumptions made when one says, "I don't feel like a part of the family anymore":

- Feeling can change reality.
- Emotions stem from environment.
- Closeness cannot be restored.

Can feeling change reality? Feelings may or may not accurately reflect fact, but feeling will never determine fact. Feelings cannot change real truth. God never told us to "feel love" for Him. People who marry or date because they feel love rarely experience successful, long-term relationships. Feelings can change based on what people eat or experience throughout the day. Feelings can change based on assumption, stress, and perception. God specifically instructed us to love Him (a verb action) when He equated and defined love as keeping and doing.

If you love Me, you will keep My commandments...
He who does not love Me does not keep My words;
and the word which you hear is not Mine, but the
Father's who sent Me.—John 14:15, 24

In the classic love chapter of the Bible, love is defined by
what it does not what it feels. True love is verb not emotion.
Feeling love does not determine the fact of love. Acting in
love, doing acts of love is love.

Love is patient, love is kind and is not jealous; love
does not brag and is not arrogant, does not act unbe-
comingly; it does not seek its own, is not provoked,
does not take into account a wrong suffered, does
not rejoice in unrighteousness, but rejoices with the
truth; bears all things, believes all things, hopes all
things, endures all things. Love never fails.—1 Cor.
13:4-8

Feeling cannot change the fact that God loves you.
Feeling cannot change the fact that God has bound you to
all other believers as family. Feeling cannot change the fact
that, functional or dysfunctional, you and your church are
family.

Feeling may or may not change reality, but can't our
feelings, and thus, our lives be affected by the church environment around us? No. Emotions do not stem directly from
environment. Emotions stem from thoughts, which stem
from beliefs, which stem from truth. What you feel is a result
of your thoughts.

When people go to a scary movie, why do they get
scared? Better, why do some people never find themselves
scared during a scary movie? There is a common factor in
these emotions: if the viewer thinks or knows it is a possible
reality, he feels the resulting emotions. That thought is based

on some belief, which is based on some truth. For example, he must believe that somewhere a guy in a hockey mask could really resurrect from a lake to wreak havoc on poor innocent people. He must have seen some fact, some truth, that this could happen, or he must have accepted some false truth.

What if the viewer accepted the following truths? Would his feelings be altered?

- There never has been one documented self-resurrection other than Jesus' and the chosen resurrected during the crucifixion.
- There has never been a killer who died in a lake and came back to life.
- There are very few serial killers.
- The probability of being the victim of a serial killer is infinitely small.
- The people are actors, and the story is a story.
- The world outside the theater is the world.

These truths would result in a set of beliefs that would leave him believing that the film was not real. The resulting thoughts would remove the fun of the movie because a horror film is not effective if you are not scared. His emotions would follow the truth, belief and thoughts.

Now take the statement "I do not feel like a part of the family anymore." What thoughts, beliefs, and truths precede this feeling? Are those thoughts, beliefs, and truths godly and accurate? How do the following absolute Christian truths impact this feeling?

- God is the loving Father of our family, and He will be that forever.

I WILL NEVER DESERT YOU, NOR WILL I
EVER FORSAKE YOU.—Heb. 13:5

• Believers are part of a family by God's action even if
they aren't good at it.

For God knew his people in advance, and he chose
them to become like his Son, so that his Son would
be the firstborn, with many brothers and sisters.—
Rom. 8:29 NLT

• Regardless of anyone else's actions, each believer
must proactively love other believers.

And God himself has commanded that we must love
not only him but our Christian brothers and sisters,
too.—1 John 4:21 (NLT)

• Closeness can easily be restored.

They devoted themselves to the apostles' teaching
and fellowship, to the breaking of bread and the
prayers.—Acts 2:42 (NRSV)

Jesus not only described love as a commitment, He did
love as a commitment. True facts require the person "not
feeling a part of the family anymore" to take immediate steps
to defeat false truth and the enemy by devoting themselves
to fellowship with believers. Christians are brothers and
sisters in Christ. This is a fact. God has joined us together,
and according to the Bible not even the gates of hell can
stand against the band of believers when they follow God. It
is fact. Believers are family whether they act like it, feel like
it, or even want it.

Once the closeness seems to be gone, if the feeling fades, can it be restored? Absolutely! Feelings were given to man by God and are not bad. To "feel" love and to "feel" family is awesome. The failure of most Christians is not understanding that God is a God of action and reaction. The action comes before the feeling. First, a person "verbs" love then he "feels" love. True love is commitment. True love does not seek the "feeling" but simply loves (verb). True love never abandons or fails. True love is exactly what God wants people to do, and only when they do love will feel love again.

This love Christians do is said by Jesus to be the single determining factor for the world to know that we are His disciples—that is, His followers.

Have this love for one another "By this all men will know that you are My disciples, if you have love for one another."—John 13:35

God did not leave believers without resources to fulfill His desires or to live a full life. He gave all believers salvation, new life, and His Spirit. We are brothers and sisters because we have one Father and can live as family because we accept the truth. Christians are not only commanded to be family—they can be family.

Now you can have sincere love for each other as brothers and sisters because you were cleansed from your sins when you accepted the truth of the Good News.—1 Pet. 1:22 (NLT)

Christians do not have to settle for this poor excuse to change churches, families, or locations. Closeness can and should be recaptured. If you leave the church, you should leave in tears of joy, not sadness and distance. The believer who is not "feeling like part of the family anymore" needs to ask, "Do I spend time with the people of the church outside of service?" Christians need to invest:

> For where your treasure is, there your heart will be also. —Luke 12:34

and spend time together, loving, being committed, and doing the things of Christ that identify them as brothers and sisters.

It does not matter how believers feel; truth matters. When believers begin to act on, believe in, and live based on the truth that they are family, they will again be able to love and find the resulting joy and sense of belonging.

6. I Am Not Being Allowed to Serve (Lead)

A church would be blessed to have a long line of servants waiting for the next opportunity to serve. What church would not want people who desired to lead? Wanting to serve and not be allowed can be frustrating. Having unfulfilled desires, especially among ministries and families, is difficult. Not being allowed to serve or lead could be a good reason to leave in a cliquish church that is closed. It might be good to leave a church that will not allow new involvement. However, it will never be good to leave for this reason if you make any of the following assumptions:

- I am qualified to serve.
- Everyone is ready when they hear the call to do.
- What I want to do is what the church should do.

What qualifies a person to serve? Is it the calling that qualifies the person? Is it some special anointing that qualifies a person to lead? There is a biblical answer. Everyone should serve other believers. Everyone should reach out to a

lost and dying world. Everyone should be given the opportunity to serve.

> Never be lazy in your work, but serve the Lord enthu-
> siastically. — Rom. 12:11 (NLT)

> But now we have been released from the Law, having
> died to that by which we were bound, so that we
> serve in newness of the Spirit and not in oldness of
> the letter. — Rom. 7:6

> Through love serve one another. — Gal. 5:13

However, not everyone is called or ready to serve in
every situation:

> Now when Simon saw that the Spirit was bestowed
> through the laying on of the apostles' hands, he offered
> them money, saying, "Give this authority to me as
> well, so that everyone on whom I lay my hands may
> receive the Holy Spirit." But Peter said to him, "May
> your silver perish with you, because you thought you
> could obtain the gift of God with money! "You have
> no part or portion in this matter, for your heart is not
> right before God." — Acts 8:18-21

> But I do not allow a woman to teach or exercise
> authority over a man, but to remain quiet. — 1 Tim.
> 2:12

Especially when it comes to leadership, not everyone
should be allowed to lead. The opportunity should be made
available but people should be qualified and their call
confirmed by the spiritual leaders in the local church. The
first servants and leaders selected in the early church were

selected based on enduring salvation, character, and confirmation of the spiritual leaders:

> Then the Twelve summoned the whole company of the disciples and said, "It would not be right for us to give up preaching about God to wait on tables. Therefore, brothers, select from among you seven men of good reputation, full of the Spirit and wisdom, whom we can appoint to this duty. But we will devote ourselves to prayer and to the preaching ministry." The proposal pleased the whole company. So they chose Stephen, a man full of faith and the Holy Spirit, and Philip, Prochorus, Nicanor, Timon, Parmenas, and Nicolaus, a proselyte from Antioch. They had them stand before the apostles, who prayed and laid their hands on them. — Acts 6:1-6 (HCSB)

Is everyone ready to lead or serve when they say they are ready? Absolutely not! The desire to serve or lead in a new way is often the catalyst that drives a person to prepare for the new responsibility.

> It is a trustworthy statement: if any man aspires to the office of overseer, it is a fine work he desires to do. An overseer, then, must be...[qualifications follow]— 1 Tim. 3:1-2

If a person simply wants to unload a truck, his preparation might be learning to be patient, to defer to others, and to work with a team. However, his first work with his new team needs to be one of learning how they do the work. It is likely they will have a system and a method to their madness. For works of more regularity or responsibility—for leadership—it is very clear that increased spiritual preparation and qualification is required. Many Christians believe they and others should simply be allowed to do anything. Many think there needs to be no training, qualification, or requirements before service. Nothing could be further from the truth. The Bible clearly illustrates that the minimum requirement is salvation, and the minimum training needs to take place under the supervision of an experienced gifted leader.

> He personally gave some to be apostles, some prophets, some evangelists, some pastors and teachers, for the training of the saints in the work of ministry, to build up the body of Christ, until we all reach unity in the faith and in the knowledge of God's Son, |growing| into a mature man with a stature measured by Christ's fullness. — Eph. 4:11-13 (HCSB)

The qualifications of the spiritual leader or minister in the church increase along with the responsibility.

> Dear brothers and sisters, not many of you should become teachers in the church, for we who teach will be judged by God with greater strictness. — James 3:1 (NLT)

The qualifications continue to increase for the servant minister:

> In the same way, deacons must be people who are respected and have integrity. They must not be heavy drinkers and must not be greedy for money. They must be committed to the revealed truths of the Christian faith and must live with a clear conscience. Before they are appointed as deacons, they should be given other responsibilities in the church as a test of their character and ability. If they do well, then they

may serve as deacons. In the same way, their wives must be respected and must not speak evil of others. They must exercise self-control and be faithful in everything they do. A deacon must be faithful to his wife, and he must manage his children and house-hold well. — 1 Tim. 3:8-12 (NLT)

And reach a peak for the spiritual leaders of the church:

For an elder must be a man whose life cannot be spoken against. He must be faithful to his wife. He must exhibit self-control, live wisely, and have a good reputation. He must enjoy having guests in his home and must be able to teach. He must not be a heavy drinker or be violent. He must be gentle, peace loving, and not one who loves money. He must manage his own family well, with children who respect and obey him. For if a man cannot manage his own household, how can he take care of God's church? An elder must not be a new Christian, because he might be proud of being chosen so soon, and the Devil will use that pride to make him fall. Also, people outside the church must speak well of him so that he will not fall into the Devil's trap and be disgraced. — 1 Tim. 3:2-7 (NLT)

So is everyone qualified for every service? No. Is everyone prepared when they sense God calling them to the work? No. Believers need to spend time preparing to be faithful, selfless, and biblically sound, qualified servants and leaders.

The church needs to be careful as well. Sometimes out of need or desire to see someone more involved the church moves a believer into a position of increased responsibility too quickly. The church and spiritual leaders need to be very careful to not confirm anyone too quickly. Acting hastily can result in disaster for the new leader. According to biblical teaching, the church leaders will be held accountable for the sins (and their haste) related to the falling of an unprepared leader who fails.

> Do not lay hands upon anyone too hastily and thereby share responsibility for the sins of others; keep yourself free from sin. — 1 Tim. 5:22

> Never be in a hurry about appointing an elder. Do not participate in the sins of others. Keep yourself pure. — 1 Tim. 5:22 (NLT)

Clearly, everyone can be called and qualified to serve, but each person must choose a life of Christianity, character, and confirmation. We should be people who are given to church life, for that is where they lead, and it is church people whom they lead. The standards will be fewer for those beginning to serve, but there are standards nonetheless. For example, people should serve according to how God has gifted them, not simply based on what they think they would like to do.

> Since we have gifts that differ according to the grace given to us, each of us is to exercise them accordingly: if prophecy, according to the proportion of his faith; if service, in his serving; or he who teaches, in his teaching...[more gifts follow] — Rom. 12:6-7

If you are thinking of leaving because you feel limited in service or leadership, first ask:

- Is there a reason I am not being allowed to serve?
- Have I really asked and listened to these people whom I think do not want me to serve?

- Have I talked to whoever is in charge?
- Have I prepared as directed?
- Could this just be an excuse?
- Do I need to grow?
- Do they know something I do not know?
- Have I been here long enough?

7. The "X" Is Much Better (or More) at "Y"

"The 'X' (thing liked) is much better (or more) at 'Y' (some other church)" is not a statement anyone wants to hear. Everyone wants their church to be great at being a church and great at what church does. Everyone wants their church to have great preaching, teaching, ministries, and outreaches. It is natural for the person who sees another church doing it better to think about going to that church.

However, this reason for leaving is more often than not a poor reason to leave, intentionally or unintentionally, based on the following assumptions:

- Everything new is better.
- If a church does a few things better, they will do everything better.
- What everyone is doing is right.

Is everything new better? Can a person be satisfied in a new place if they are always looking for something new? When will the new get old? Every new thing is not better, but, even more revealing, nothing is new.

That which has been is that which will be, and that which has been done is that which will be done. o there is nothing new under the sun. —Eccles. 1:9

One denomination begins contemporary worship believing they have found the "crown jewels" of worship, while the denomination that was contemporary finds beauty and truth in returning to the roots of ancient Christian hymns revived for worship. The storytelling, topical preacher is greatly desired, and his humor and wit are enjoyed for a season until, for lack of knowledge, the people demand to know more about the Bible as a whole. Activity-based ministries are the rage in one genre that is moving from service to have a little more fun, while the genre that was activity-based is moving back to service of the community. There is nothing new. There are only things new to a person's perspective.

Life goes in cycles, and old styles return to be seen as new. In the flesh, man desires the new thing or, better, that which appears new. It is the natural part of man, not the spiritual, that craves newness, desires more, and always looks to the next thing. It is like a mid-life man who thinks, "Well, that 20-year-old is just more exciting" and leaves his wife and kids. Everyone knows the new girl won't be exciting soon enough. She, too, will wrinkle.

Things may not always be what was dreamed of or thought of as people mature in churches and in the Lord. The flesh will always crave, and the common enemy will always plant the seed of what we should or could have. What is so new will become old.

Does a church that does a few things better do everything better? No. Can a church pray better? Can a church truly worship better? Can a church read God's Word better? Can a church love better? Certainly, people using this reason are talking about style and method, not principle. The true qualities of a church are pass-fail qualities: that is, the church either does them or does not have these qualities. There is no better or worse in these core qualities, and people leaving because "X" is better at "Y" are not referring to these core qualities. If the people leaving had issues with the core qualities, they would say something definite, such as, "This church is disobedient and does not read the Bible. I am going to a church that reads the Bible."

However, in regard to style and method, it is unlikely any church does everything better than every other church. It follows that in leaving to get the thing that is better, there will be some concession as the new church does something less well than the old church. Which means, eventually, the one leaving the old church will, knowingly or unknowingly, long for what the old church did better. It would be great if the person realizing another church does "Y" better would help his church improve at "Y" instead of moving to consume from that better church.

Is what everyone is doing right? Is the latest rage the best thing? Just because "X" church seems successful in numbers or method does not mean that what "X" is doing is right. Likewise, it does not mean what "X" is doing is wrong. Everyone doing anything will never make the anything definitively right.

Scripture often refers to the few who remained faithful, the few who were wise, or the few who remained unstained by the world.

> Wise speech is rarer and more valuable than gold and rubies. — Prov. 20:15 (NLT)

People who say that "X" is better or does more of "Y" are often focusing on how something shows or feels instead of seeking what is best or needed. For all of the flash, attraction, and seeming success, the apostles and the Spirit did not seem to put much emphasis on exciting methods or what they could do best to draw people to salvation and learning. Instead, the focus seemed to be on the sufficiency of Christ alone.

For Christ did not send me to baptize, but to preach the gospel, not in cleverness of speech, so that the cross of Christ would not be made void. — 1 Cor. 1:17

And when I came to you, brethren, I did not come with superiority of speech or of wisdom, proclaiming to you the testimony of God. For I determined to know nothing among you except Jesus Christ, and Him crucified. — 1 Cor. 2:1-2

For we did not follow cleverly devised tales when we made known to you the power and coming of our Lord Jesus Christ, but we were eyewitnesses of His majesty. — 2 Pet. 1:16

Christians need to seek to be at church, in corporate fellowship and worship, for the essential reasons. We need to stay where we are called and help each church be the best instead of flocking to what seems better with an immature consumer mentality.

8. I Am Not Sure I Agree with "X"

Everyone hates it when things just don't feel in sync. Everyone hates feeling that something isn't right. It should bother Christians when their brothers or sisters have to struggle with thoughts like, "I don't know what it is. Something just doesn't feel right" or "I just don't think I agree with 'X.'" However, believers need to know that changing churches will never solve the problem. "I am not sure I agree" is a weak, poor reason to leave. It leads people into sin, and it carries with it some poor assumptions:

- What a person agrees with is the basis for church selection.
- Feeling ambiguous is something that can be changed by circumstance.
- God is a god who does not give clear direction.

Many poor reasons to leave could cause a person to sin but this reason will always result in sin. Your church may be doing something wrong, your feeling might be correct, God may want you to leave but you are doomed to be wrong if this is your reason for leaving. Why? Romans 14:23 teaches that "everything that is not from faith is sin" (Rom. 14:23, HCSB).

This intricate passage explains one of the simplest, clearest messages in Christian living. There are three ways to sin. The first way to sin is to do something that God has said not to do. James 4:17 reveals that the second way to sin is to not do something that God has said to do. The third way to sin is to do something in doubt. The word "faith" as used in Romans 14:23 means believing beyond a shadow of doubt that God told you to do something. So another, more wordy, rendering of the passage could be "everything that a person does that he is not absolutely sure is what God wants him to do is sin" (my paraphrase).

Throughout the Bible God reveals, teaches, and instructs His people about sin. Sin is choosing anything not of God. If a person is not certain that God wants him to do what he is getting ready to do, even if he guesses correctly, he will sin in doing it. God wants us to be sure we are choosing Him. If we aren't sure, then we aren't choosing God but instead we are choosing our best guess. Guessing in Christianity is sin. The phrase "I am not sure..." dooms any believer to sin.

The first poor assumption is that a believer must agree with everything for the church to be the right church for him. Is agreement the basis for church selection? Definitely not. Perhaps God has called a believer to a church to help it grow, and therefore the believer should not agree with everything. Perhaps the believer is immature and needs to grow, and as a child on the matter, he will not yet be able to agree. Being disagreeable is wrong, but disagreeing is not wrong. Disagreeing is often the beginning of spiritual growth. The solution to disagreeing is to find harmony and one answer. After all:

> We know that there is only one God, the Father, who created everything, and we exist for him. And there is only one Lord, Jesus Christ, through whom God made everything and through whom we have been given life. — 1 Cor. 8:6 (NLT)

And as Paul taught:

> I urge Euodia and I urge Syntyche to agree in the Lord. Yes, I also ask you, true partner, to help these women who have contended for the gospel at my side, along with Clement and the rest of my co-workers whose names are in the book of life. — Phil. 4:2-3 (HCSB)

The church is family, a team, a group, and a single unit. Believers might find themselves disagreeing with one another, even if they are standing side by side with the same goals in the same church. The call is to work through the disagreement and continue to stand together. Only the immature cuts and runs from disagreement. He does not understand that in resolving the disagreement he saves either himself or his brother. He does not understand that leaving with disagreement dooms one party to certain death. Nonetheless, disagreement and agreement are not the basis of selecting churches.

Can changing geographical location create clarity? Does doubt flee from people's lives if they change their circumstances? Doubt is dangerous. Romans 14:23 addresses the sin that comes from thinking and guessing. Even more, James reveals another danger of doubt:

> Now if any of you lacks wisdom, he should ask God, who gives to all generously and without criticizing, and it will be given to him. But let him ask in faith without doubting. For the doubter is like the surging sea, driven and tossed by the wind. That person should not expect to receive anything from the Lord. An indecisive man is unstable in all his ways. — James 1:5-8 (HCSB)

The one who is not sure, who does not know, is like the surging sea. God says the doubter "should not expect to receive anything from the Lord." Making life decisions based on uncertainty is dangerous, but, as James reveals, there is little chance of hearing a clear answer while doubting. It is certain that changing the geographic location will not answer the questions. Believers need answers that they can be sure of so that they don't err in the future. Doubt flees when faith is exercised in the heart. Doubt flees when you are certain of what God teaches or wants. Circumstances will never change your heart. Only God can remove doubt.

Is God a god who doesn't give clear direction? The person who prepares to leave when he isn't really sure that he agrees is a person who does not understand God. God is a god of clear direction and detail. The Bible teaches, and illustrates in the lives of believers, that God will provide very clear direction and detail to people who wait on His direction and are committed to living according to that direction.

"I am not sure I agree with 'X'" is easily diagnosed as a poor reason to leave because of the phrase "I am not sure."

9. I Can't Learn Anything Else Here

Some people may leave because they are not sure if they agree, but many people leave because they believe they have learned everything. Most people can understand this feeling, thinking of a time when they simply weren't learning anything new while sitting in a service or class. It is inevitable. Unless a church separates all of the new Christians from all of the old Christians and all of the young from the aged, certainly someone is going to hear a duplicate message or lesson from God's Word. Given that separating the mature believers from the immature believers is unbiblical (Romans 15:4, Hebrews 10:24, Titus 2:3-4, and other passages), there must be another option. The people and leaders must accept that some truths must be taught to new generations and might only serve as reminders to the previous generations. The learned listener must allow the message to remind and revive him while rejoicing in what the new generation is learning for the first time. This is the call of the mature.

Give instruction to a wise man and he will be still wiser, teach a righteous man and he will increase his learning.—Prov. 9:9

A wise man will hear and increase in learning, and a man of understanding will acquire wise counsel, To understand a proverb and a figure, The words of the wise and their riddles.—Prov. 1:5-6

But isn't there a time when it is good to leave to go to a new place so you can learn more? Isn't that why we have colleges, seminaries, and the like? Can't one church offer more spiritual food than another?

The desire to learn and to grow in God's Word and Christian living is admirable. No one should be denied that right, and the church must provide that opportunity. However, there are some dangerous assumptions and misunderstandings surrounding the person who says, "I am leaving because I can't learn anything here anymore."

- Learning is what Christianity is about.
- "Getting" is the primary activity of the learner.
- Others are supposed to teach.

Is learning what Christianity is about? No. Christianity is all about living. Christianity is all about applying. Christianity is about a relationship with God. It has been this way since the beginning. God's plan has always been that man would walk with Him in relationship. Churches reduce worship service to some great songs and some great teaching when the people should be encouraged to engage and worship God. Teaching is for sanctification, and sanctification is for perfection, and perfection is for living. Teaching and learning only facilitate the believer to walk well with God. God never intended for man to be intelligent about Him. God's desire was for man to be changed by His wisdom. There should come a point in time when you become learned; that is, you have learned the truth and have adjusted to the truth by applying it to your life. The need to learn never goes away, but the amount you have to learn reduces with each lesson truly learned. It is natural that the mature believer is going to need to learn less. So what happens when people learn more and more and have less and less to learn? First, they should become doers. Doers are people equipped to serve other believers and to follow God's commands.

But prove yourselves doers of the word, and not merely hearers who delude themselves. —James 1:22

He is the one who gave these gifts to the church: the apostles, the prophets, the evangelists, and the pastors and teachers. Their responsibility is to equip God's people to do his work and build up the church, the body of Christ, until we come to such unity in our faith and knowledge of God's Son that we will be mature and full grown in the Lord, measuring up to the full stature of Christ. Then we will no longer be like children, forever changing our minds about what we believe because someone has told us something different or because someone has cleverly lied to us and made the lie sound like the truth. Instead, we will hold to the truth in love, becoming more and more in every way like Christ, who is the head of his body, the church. Under his direction, the whole body is fitted together perfectly. As each part does its own special work, it helps the other parts grow, so that the whole body is healthy and growing and full of love. — Eph. 4:11-16 (NLT)

People who are not doers cannot say they have nothing left to learn. People who are doers need to take the next step. Notice the end of the passage in Ephesians 4, where it is written "it [the mature part] helps the other parts grow."

Is getting the primary activity of the learner? According to Hebrews 5:12-14, learning should result in people who then teach:

For though by this time you ought to be teachers, you have need again for someone to teach you the elementary principles of the oracles of God, and you have come to need milk and not solid food. For everyone who partakes only of milk is not accustomed to the word of righteousness, for he is an infant. But solid food is for the mature, who because of practice have their senses trained to discern good and evil. — Heb. 5:12-14

God says that "by this time you ought to be teachers," but you still need someone to teach you the basics. "Getting" is the initial act of the learner, but it is not the mature act of the learner. Learners advance in knowledge and wisdom to become those who give knowledge. The more you learn, the more you are responsible to convey to others that which you have heard.

Go therefore and make disciples of all the nations, baptizing them in the name of the Father and the Son and the Holy Spirit, teaching them to observe all that I commanded you; and lo, I am with you always, even to the end of the age. — Matt. 28:19-20

What I tell you now in the darkness, shout abroad when daybreak comes. What I whisper in your ears, shout from the housetops for all to hear! — Matt. 10:27 (NLT)

Many teachers have said, "Wow. I learned so much more preparing to teach than I ever did learning from a teacher." Teachers must live the truth, know the truth, and learn well enough to articulate the truth to others. The objective of learning for the parent should be to teach the child. The objective for the spouse is to complete the other spouse. The objective for the Christian is to help those who have not learned. The objective for all is to teach out of experience and application.

Is everyone called to teach? Should only the one who speaks well teach? The Bible teaches that God is the one who will give the words to teachers and leaders.

Then Moses said to the LORD, "Please, Lord, I have never been eloquent, neither recently nor in time past, nor since You have spoken to Your servant; for I am slow of speech and slow of tongue." The LORD said to him, "Who has made man's mouth? Or who makes him mute or deaf, or seeing or blind? Is it not I, the LORD? "Now then go, and I, even I, will be with your mouth, and teach you what you are to say." — Exod. 4:10-12

But when you are arrested and stand trial, don't worry about what to say in your defense. Just say what God tells you to. Then it is not you who will be speaking, but the Holy Spirit. — Mark 13:11 (NLT)

As well, the Bible teaches that every Christian participates in the teaching and learning as they grow:

Older women likewise are to be reverent in their behavior, not malicious gossips nor enslaved to much wine, teaching what is good, so that they may encourage the young women to love their husbands, to love their children, to be sensible, pure, workers at home, kind, being subject to their own husbands, so that the word of God will not be dishonored. — Titus 2:3-5

Even parents and the people of God are responsible to teach their own children:

You shall teach them diligently to your sons and shall talk of them when you sit in your house and when you walk by the way and when you lie down and when you rise up. — Deut. 6:7

If you leave saying, "I can't learning anything else here," you show how little that you really have learned. People making this claim inadvertently look down on the family around them and say that they are neither good enough to learn from nor good enough to teach. Neither great teachers nor great learners will use this reason to leave.

10. I Want to Get "X" Involved

There is no greater desire than to get family members, spouses, or friends involved in Christianity. Everyone wants the people they love to find a full Christian life and joy. This seemingly good reason to change churches, however, rarely achieves the goal of the one leaving. The grandkids may go once or twice, and the grown son may show up for Easter, but little new commitment is found. The student attends excitedly until he finds out the new youth group also has its own weaknesses. The husband tries the new church and then falls back into his old ways during the football season. In interview results, rarely does the one "left for" really want the one leaving to leave.

There are fundamental reasons a person leaving to get "X" involved will, most likely, never see their dream achieved. The logic of changing geographic location to get "X" involved is flawed because of the following assumptions:

- If "X" likes the surroundings, "X" will come to church and be changed.
- It is my responsibility to get "X" to go to church.
- I am showing sincerity by moving, and "X" will respond.

Will "X" come if "X" likes the surroundings? Possibly, but a better question follows: "Will 'X' follow Christ?" If a person finds a church that is loving, familiar, exciting, or inspiring, he will often attend church services. However, pastors and growth consultants know there is no single type of church that attracts people who are disconnected from God. Instead, it is most often people who are excited about God, or at least their church, that attract disconnected people. You must never forget that it is Jesus who adds to the church:

> I [Jesus] will build my church, and all the powers of hell will not conquer it. — Matt. 16:18 (NLT)

And all of the power to change lives is not in the praise band but in the Good News of Jesus Christ:

> For I am not ashamed of the gospel, for it is the power of God for salvation to everyone who believes, to the Jew first and also to the Greek. — Rom. 1:16

And the Bible:

> All Scripture is inspired by God and is profitable for teaching, for rebuking, for correcting, for training in righteousness, so that the man of God may be complete, equipped for every good work. — 2 Tim. 3:16-17 (HCSB)

In the final analysis, it is always Jesus, the Good News, and the Bible that attract and truly change a person's life. There is nothing man can do: no song that can be sung, no fellowship that can be had, and no attraction so powerful that it will forever change the hearts of men. The one leaving to get "X" involved needs to be careful to be more concerned about the eternal destination of "X" instead of the church attendance of "X." Instead of leaving their church, people need to share the Good News with those whom they care about. It is far more effective.

How then will they call on Him in whom they have not believed? How will they believe in Him whom they have not heard? And how will they hear without a preacher?—Rom. 10:14

Is it a grandparent's responsibility to get the grandchild to go to church? Is it the parents' responsibility to get their teen or child to church? Is it the wife's responsibility to get the husband to go church? Is it the parent's responsibility to get a grown child to attend church? Any Christian having biblical responsibility for another person is responsible to discipline the person, giving him every opportunity for success and faith in God. If a child or teen is not involved in church, a parent is charged with the responsibility to get her to church. Parents should be positive and hope for a great experience, but parents are the boss and need to say, "We are going. You are going. I have prayed. They teach the Bible. This church is where we are called. Get dressed." The Bible says nothing about the child liking the learning but rather teaches that when the child gets older and wiser he will thank the parent and walk in the right path.

Train up a child in the way he should go, even when he is old he will not depart from it.—Prov. 22:6

As for grandparents, the charge is the same. There should be no orphans among the church, and that includes spiritual orphans. Uncles, aunts, brothers, sisters, and grandparents, though not officially the authority over the child, should do everything possible to teach and train the child personally and at church.

It is not the wife's responsibility to get her husband to go to church. In fact, the Bible teaches the wife to not nag her husband but rather let him see what Jesus has done in her life. This practice is the command of God and works again and again.

> In the same way, you wives, be submissive to your own husbands so that even if any of them are disobedient to the word, they may be won without a word by the behavior of their wives, as they observe your chaste and respectful behavior. — 1 Pet. 3:1-2

It is honorable for a parent to reach out and to even be willing to change churches because they long for their grown child to attend church, but there is no command to do so. The Bible teaches that adults are accountable for themselves. In fact, the Bible is pretty clear that adults have to be adults and that parents need to let go (e.g., Gen. 2:24). Probably the best approach is to have a great and fun Christian life that is healthy and attractive to the adult child. Stability and a productive walk will make an impact.

Will a lost child, friend, or spouse see true sincerity if you leave your church to try to reach them? Without a doubt, your actions will show human sincerity, but it silently shows something much more dangerous. Leaving for this reason shows that the one leaving is willing to risk wandering from where God told him to attend. It shows disloyalty to his church family. Leaving for this reason makes no sense. It casts off the very picture of fellowship that is desired for the child, friend, or spouse. Believers should be proud of and committed to being part of a congregation. The very act of being willing to leave this way raises a question about the value of church life. Even worse, it shows people that it is okay to choose loved ones before God.

The church needs to remain sensitive to those who really believe leaving might get their spouse, child, or friend to come to church. People get desperate and are willing to do almost anything to reach someone they love. However, false hope is no hope at all, and leaving to get "X" involved still comes up short of the one great reason to leave a church.

Chapter 4

Leaving Well
Making the Righteous Departure

There are least ten good reasons to leave that could easily become ten great reasons to stay. There is one great reason to stay. There are least ten really poor reasons to leave. There is one great reason to leave. There are ways to leave well, and there are ways to leave poorly. It's time for the church and individuals to embrace a solution that ushers in an era of the righteous departure.

Living well before leaving is the solution that the church needs. Living well in the church will cause the people to leave well when it comes time to go. Living well will cause the church to champion good departures. Living well is the solution, but there is another means of help in the battle to stop the cycle of poor departures: understanding the battle plans that Satan, our common enemy, has against the church. There is something much greater than personal choice behind it all. Leaving and coming poorly is part of an age-old battle. The stakes are incredible.

It is interesting and important to answer, "Why do people leave poorly?" It will be important to look at how people live well before they leave. However, the first question to ask in order to understand Satan's advantage and plan for dividing the church is this: "What types of people leave poorly?"

Ultimately, all types of people leave poorly. The rich, the poor, the highly educated, the less educated, the serious, the happy, the deep, and the shallow can all leave poorly. Leaving poorly is indiscriminate of age, sex, or creed.

There is one common denominator with everyone who leaves poorly: regardless of their reason or claim, they choose themselves over God and the church in the process of leaving. They may be leaving poorly out of ignorance, but their ignorance is based on choosing themselves and their schedules over studying the Word of God regarding the church and their role.

The key to understanding leaving poorly is to understand it will always violate "Love the Lord your God with all your heart, soul and mind and love your neighbor as yourself" (Matt. 22:37-40). Leaving poorly will always treat your brother or sister in Christ as a stranger or an enemy. Leaving poorly will always have a factor of selfishness. The one leaving poorly is blind to God's design of the body of Christ and how Christians are to live together.

Typically, those who leave well give to the body of Christ and improve it while those who leave poorly take from the body of Christ. Perhaps unknowingly, the one who leaves poorly plays directly into the enemy's plan to divide and conquer believers and the church.

The Enemy's Battle Plan

The person leaving poorly is often misguided, selfish, or immature; however, these reasons may not be the only reasons for departures. There is a spiritual enemy—a real enemy—that each believer and the church faces daily. Though the enemy's war is with God, dividing the church is often his primary objective.

First, though, believers must understand this war. Satan's single goal is not to shame or destroy the lives of people but to shame God and steal God's glory by getting people to choose themselves instead of God.

The second and third chapters of Ephesians teach this great truth. Paul was sent to these people to share the Good News that God loved them and wanted to forgive and restore them. The people chose God.

> Now you who are not Jewish are not foreigners or strangers any longer, but are citizens together with God's holy people. You belong to God's family.— Eph. 2:19-20 (NCV)

Later, Paul tells why God gave him this great calling to share the Good News. He tells why it is so important when people choose God.

> And God gave me the work of telling all people about the plan for his secret, which has been hidden in him since the beginning of time. He is the One who created everything. His purpose was that through the church all the rulers and powers in the heavenly world will now know God's wisdom, which has so many forms. This agrees with the purpose God had since the beginning of time, and he carried out his plan through Christ Jesus our Lord.—Eph. 3:9-11 (NCV)

Every time people choose God, His righteousness, and His redemption, God's majesty is demonstrated to everyone and everything. Likewise, His majesty is demonstrated every time believers choose God over themselves. According to Jesus,

> The thief [the enemy, Satan] comes only to steal and
> kill and destroy; I came that they may have life, and
> have it abundantly. —John 10:10

Satan's opposition to God is demonstrated as he tries
to steal the majesty of God by getting man to choose "not
God." The book of Job records a great example of this battle
that Satan is trying to wage against God through the choices
of people.

> Then the LORD said to Satan, "Have you noticed my
> servant Job? No one else on earth is like him. He is an
> honest and innocent man, honoring God and staying
> away from evil." But Satan answered the LORD,
> "Job honors God for a good reason. You have put a
> wall around him, his family, and everything he owns.
> You have blessed the things he has done. His flocks
> and herds are so large they almost cover the land.
> But reach out your hand and destroy everything he
> has, and he will curse you to your face."—Job 1:8-11
> NCV

Satan's single goal is to show God that He is not God and
that man will not choose Him if given the proper incentive.
Unfortunately, Satan is successful in his battle more often
than not. Even believers continue to choose their ways over
God's commands.

How does the church and poor departures figure into this
war? First, the church, when assembled in all its glory and
design, is Satan's enemy on earth.

> I also say to you that you are Peter, and upon this
> rock I will build My church; and the gates of Hades
> will not overpower it. —Matt. 16:18

Second, many people leave churches poorly because they have become the casualties as Satan tries to divide and conquer the church—his greatest enemy on earth. Satan understands warfare. If he can keep the church focused on its own selfish desires, keep it uneducated, keep it constantly shifting and changing, he can destroy the foundation of his greatest earthly enemy.

Satan's greatest tactic is taking advantage of man's greatest weakness—sin living in man's flesh. Choosing God and ignoring the desires and demands of the flesh and this earthly life takes great discipline. Paul understood this principle when he wrote about all believers:

> So now I am no longer the one doing it, but it is sin living in me. For I know that nothing good lives in me, that is, in my flesh. For the desire to do what is good is with me, but there is no ability to do it. For I do not do the good that I want to do, but I practice the evil that I do not want to do. Now if I do what I do not want, I am no longer the one doing it, but it is the sin that lives in me. So I discover this principle: when I want to do good, evil is with me.—Rom. 7:17-21 (HCSB)

The common enemy knows man must choose God, His ways, and His people before himself. Satan knows how difficult it can be to choose well. The common enemy is great at feeding man's humanity. He uses our greatest weakness to achieve two purposes at once. When Christians choose themselves, he shames God, and he divides the church.

Though Satan is behind all the poor church moves, he does not really care about individual people or their happiness. Man is hopelessly deluded into thinking this battle between good and evil is about him. Does Satan want men to be miserable? Satan doesn't care whether people are happy or not. He just does not want people to do good because good is defined by God. Satan does not care if man is happy, sad, rich, poor, wise, or dumb as long as man does not choose God.

In regard to the topic of church, Satan is going to try to destroy and divide the church. He can read the Bible and knows the truth:

I will build my church, and all the powers of hell will not conquer it. — Matt. 16:18 (NLT)

Leaving poorly always divides, subtracts, and takes away from the healthy church family of Christ. In the end, there are only two reasons people leave poorly:

• They are not saved, or
• The enemy wants it this way and wins their hearts.

If people are not saved, the church should not be surprised when those people leave poorly. Little can be done other than to graciously restate the Good News of Jesus Christ and His promise of unity and peace.

In regard to believers, many churches need a wake-up call. The church needs to read the preceding paragraphs and realize there is a common enemy. The church needs to realize that the immature or selfish believer is not hurting its work, but rather the glory of God, when he leaves poorly. What Christian in his right mind would want to leave poorly? If a Christian knew the enemy was behind his poor departure, he would be scared to death. No one in his right mind would continue down a course if their mortal enemy said, "Look, I am trying to mess you over, so follow this course of action that looks good to you or seems to overcome your frustration. In the end, though, I, your mortal enemy, am going to steal your King's glory, divide you from your family, and delude you into thinking it will all be better, when really it will not."

Evil, the opposite of good, can seem attractive because it feeds selfishness, which is man's greatest temptation. The enemy is so elusive and so good at what he does. His expertise, coupled with man's desire to find an excuse to do what he wants to do, results in men's hearts becoming selfish or misguided. God may not even protect the heart of people who know of His glory but choose His enemy.

> For even though they knew God, they did not honor Him as God or give thanks, but they became futile in their speculations, and their foolish heart was darkened. Professing to be wise, they became fools, and exchanged the glory of the incorruptible God for an image in the form of corruptible man and of birds and four-footed animals and crawling creatures.
>
> Therefore God gave them over in the lusts of their hearts to impurity, so that their bodies would be dishonored among them. For they exchanged the truth of God for a lie, and worshiped and served the creature rather than the Creator, who is blessed forever. Amen.—Rom. 1:21-25

The enemy derives glory in stealing God's glory and destroying His church. The enemy wins with every poor departure. How can believers defeat Satan at his own game? How can believers stop falling in the battle and reclaim the glory of their God? Believers have at their disposal two great remedies with which to defeat division of the church and believers.

The Question Strategy: Satan Spurs Poor Departures

One of Satan's great weapons to distract, divide, and de-motivate Christians is getting them to ask questions that do not need to be asked. The enemy strives to get people to question what they already know to be true. Remember, divided Christians equate to a divided church, which equates to Satan weakening his opponent and stealing God's glory. Since the beginning of time, Satan has been using this great weapon, getting people to desire unnecessary information. Eve's situation is an example:

> The woman said to the serpent, "We may eat the fruit from the trees in the garden. But about the fruit of the tree in the middle of the garden, God said, 'You must not eat it or touch it, or you will die.'
> "No! You will not die," the serpent said to the woman. "In fact, God knows that when you eat it your eyes will be opened and you will be like God, knowing good and evil." —Gen. 3:2-5 (HCSB)

The enemy's greatest tactic is to get Christians to question what they already know to be true. Eve had a great life and a great relationship with God. She had everything she needed. Without a doubt, there were things that Eve did not know and for good cause. Eve knew that life was good, and she knew that fundamental to life was that she not eat from one tree. Eve had that clear direction that all followers of God long to have. God gave her everything she needed and gave her clear instruction on what to do and how to keep all that was good. Eve knew by experience what was true, but Satan was able to get her to question the truth she knew and believe a myth he created.

Christianity is based on great wisdom that is very broad and very simple. The fundamentals of the Christian life are so easy that children can live according to them without great explanation. The questions of the young do not shake the longstanding foundations of wisdom nor challenge God in an inappropriate way. The old find a depth of understanding and truth that escapes words to describe it. However, each group is experiencing the same simple but very broad, everlasting truth. Christianity is not a fool's life. Christianity does not require blinders to prevent the believer from seeing something better. Christianity is convincing and reforming in and of itself.

People should ask what they need to know about God and accept the unchanging truth with which He responds. People should study the Bible, unlocking the depth within its simple truths. Questions will never defeat believers, and intelligence will only confirm God's direction as the best direction. Satan is well aware of the resiliency of truth; therefore, he seeks only to create doubt. He does not try to refute truth directly because his work would quickly become evident. Instead he whispers, "Are you sure? Look at those believers" and prompts thoughts like, "If we are doing this at God's bidding, why is it so hard now?" He raises questions that are easily answered by circumstantial evidence, other people, or himself.

How unrighteous is it for a man to wake up one morning and ask, "Am I happy in this marriage? God, was I really supposed to get married? Should I stay here?" The better question would be, "God, I am troubled in my heart about my marriage. I am lacking the luster. Will You help me honor my vows, inspire me, and fix whatever problems there might be in me? Will You send Your Spirit to empower me to keep my commitment to You?" How crazy would it be for a person to wake up each day and say, "God, I know You gave me the job at the plant, but I just wanted to ask You today, again, do You really want me working there?"

Some questions simply do not need to be asked. Some questions are more likely to be answered by the enemy or by others than God. Many of the questions that shouldn't be asked are asked by people trying to get God to give them what they want. The Israelites provide a great example of this in the Old Testament. In the end, God even gave them what they asked for. However, what He gave was not what He wanted for them.

Finally, the leaders of Israel met at Ramah to discuss the matter with Samuel. "Look," they told him, "you are now old, and your sons are not like you. Give us a king like all the other nations have."

Samuel was very upset with their request and went to the LORD for advice. "Do as they say," the LORD replied, "for it is me they are rejecting, not you. They don't want me to be their king any longer. Ever since I brought them from Egypt they have continually forsaken me and followed other gods. And now they are giving you the same treatment. Do as they ask, but solemnly warn them about how a king will treat them."

So Samuel passed on the LORD's warning to the people. "This is how a king will treat you," Samuel said. "The king will draft your sons into his army and make them run before his chariots. Some will be commanders of his troops, while others will be slave laborers. Some will be forced to plow in his fields and harvest his crops, while others will make his weapons and chariot equipment. The king will take your daughters from you and force them to cook and bake and make perfumes for him. He will take away the best of your fields and vineyards and olive groves and give them to his own servants. He will take a tenth of your harvest and distribute it among his officers and attendants. He will want your male and female slaves and demand the finest of your cattle and donkeys for his own use. He will demand a tenth of your flocks, and you will be his slaves. When that day comes, you will beg for relief from this king you are demanding, but the LORD will not help you."

But the people refused to listen to Samuel's warning. "Even so, we still want a king," they said. "We want to be like the nations around us. Our king will govern us and lead us into battle."

So Samuel told the LORD what the people had said, and the LORD replied, "Do as they say, and give them a king." — 1 Sam. 8:4-22 (NLT)

For the Christian, the enemy's question is the question that demonstrates a lack of faith. The dooming question is the question that indicates that the asker as already distant from the one who has the answer. "God, should I really be here, at this church?" is a valid question, but it is also a question that indicates a lack of ongoing communication and maturity. If a person doesn't know if he should be at a church, if he has not already heard and, in faith, known that he should be there, what is the likelihood of him hearing a clear answer to whether he should leave?

The better question might be, "God, the last thing I heard was to be here, and for some reason I am doubting that direction. Could You please restore the faith for me to know I heard from You?" Another great question would be, "Why am I not sure of You? Is there an issue with me that would deny You and Your glory?"

When someone asks an unanswerable question, the void already existing combined with the distance from their faith, is easily filled with input from people and the false truths of the enemy. When a seemingly faithless question is challenged, most people say, "Well, we can ask anything of God.

He loves us." God does love people, and He wants them to ask Him about everything. James 1:5-8 teaches,

> But if any of you lacks wisdom, let him ask of God, who gives to all generously and without reproach, and it will be given to him. —James 1:5

However, God also reserves the right to not answer the person who is not going to listen to Him or follow the direction He gives.

> But he must ask in faith without any doubting, for the one who doubts is like the surf of the sea, driven and tossed by the wind. For that man ought not to expect that he will receive anything from the Lord, being a double-minded man, unstable in all his ways. — James 1:6-8

People must ask in faith and must have total trust in God. The person asking in faith is committed before hearing the answer to absolutely and immediately follow the answer that will be given. The above scripture is clear; if man asks and is not absolutely sure he will do whatever God directs, he should not expect to get anything. The one who is not committed in his heart, knowing and doing the will of God, is called "unstable in all his ways."

Defeating the Question Strategy with Servanthood

Servanthood is God's natural protection against this great weapon of the enemy—asking questions that cannot be answered or do not need to be asked. God called us to be servants. Servants are people who do what they heard last until they hear again. Servants do not ask a lot of procedural questions even though they may probe the depths of their master's wisdom. The servant principle says, "What did I hear last from God that I was sure was God? I am going to do that until I hear another direction." The servant principle is not about doing but being.

> I assure you: A slave is not greater than his master, and a messenger is not greater than the one who sent him. If you know these things, you are blessed if you do them. —John 13:16-17 (HCSB)

A servant denies Satan's great weapon by not asking questions that shouldn't be asked and choosing truth. A servant returns to and continues the last thing spoken from the master and does not vary from that goal until the master speaks clearly again. The master is capable of making himself heard, and the servant is willing to wait. If in doubt, the servant asks for confirmation of what he was doing and continues to do. Jesus lived this way while on earth.

> Therefore Jesus answered and was saying to them, "Truly, truly, I say to you, the Son can do nothing of Himself, unless it is something He sees the Father doing; for whatever the Father does, these things the Son also does in like manner." —John 5:19

Why would any servant think he could surpass Jesus' model of living on earth? Christians should be servant driven and:

- Demand truth to be their standard and give themselves to nothing less.
- Do what they know to be consistent with God's truth.
- Do only what they are convinced that God has told them to do.

- Recall the truth of God's direction when the enemy or their mind raises questions.
- Do what the truth and God's related call directs until He calls again.

Believers have given themselves to some truth of God. If they had not, they would not be called Christians. However, it is common for men to forget the beginning of their commitment to, devotion to, and dependence on God's truth. The entire history of the Israelites reflects this cycle of commitment, forgetfulness, and rejection. Christians can be just as fickle:

But those who fail to develop these virtues are blind or, at least, very shortsighted. They have already forgotten that God has cleansed them from their old life of sin. — 2 Pet. 1:9 (NLT)

But I have this against you: you have abandoned the love lyou hadl at first. Remember then how far you have fallen; repent, and do the works you did at first. Otherwise, I will come to you and remove your lampstand from its place — unless you repent. — Rev. 2:4-5 (HCSB)

Too often, believers act on what they are sure God is saying, when they really are not so sure. They are like teenagers who want something to be true rather than older people who know what is true. The test for any believer saying "God has told me" should be that he is willing to die on a cross to complete the task.

The common enemy's war is against God. His greatest weapon to distract, divide, and de-motivate Christians is getting them to ask questions that do not need to be asked because they foolishly question what they already know to be true. But there is another weapon, one of equal merit, that he uses in the battle to divide and conquer the church.

The "Red Light" Strategy: Satan Supports Poor Departures

While the first great weapon wants people to ask inappropriate and unnecessary questions, there is yet another great weapon in Satan's arsenal. Using this weapon, Satan seeks to get people to make poor decisions while having them believe that they are doing God's bidding, believing that God gave them direction.

The weapon is a faulty decision-making method. Promoted by man and likely created by Satan himself, this method appears so correct that almost every believer has fallen prey to its destruction at some point. It is the "Red Light" method of making decisions, and it normally has these points:

- I have not heard from God, but I have been asking.
- God doesn't want us to be idle.
- I need to make a decision.
- God loves me enough to keep me from making a mistake.
- I need direction.
- God can give me a sign.

The premise of this idea is that a person wants to follow God and has some answer or direction that he requires. Not absolutely sure of God's direction, the person takes off on the journey saying, "God, if this is not what You want, stop me. Give me a sign. Give me a red light. I am going to begin to move forward. Show me which way." This unknowing believer fails to understand that moving forward looking for the "red light" is infinitely dangerous, immature, and not biblically supported.

You may have played a childhood game called "Red Light, Green Light." In this game, there is one traffic director who uses the simple commands "red light" for stop and "green light" for go. The other children line up away from the traffic director and move toward him as he gives the command "green light." The objective is to get to the director without getting tricked. The director's only strategy is to trick the children into going when they should stop. Though the children can find themselves disqualified during the game, they understand more importantly that they are immediately disqualified if they begin before the director says "green light."

Believers need to understand that they, too, are not following God if they begin without a green light. The truth of Romans 14:23 rings true again and again.

Everything that is not from faith is sin. — Rom. 14:23 (HCSB)

Doing something, guessing something that you are not sure of, is one of the three ways to sin.

No pilot would ever take off without the green light. Every race car driver knows disqualification lies on the other side of jumping the green flag. Only in the concept of the spiritual — and for this context, Christianity and the church — can a person delude himself into thinking that looking for the red light is a good answer.

The desperate red light seeker admits his own inability to hear from and understand God when he says, "God, if it is not what You want, then stop me." Interestingly, this statement is most often made after asking an inappropriate question that God has not answered or will not answer. So, not hearing a clear answer, the believer now resorts to trial and error, looking for God to stop him if he is wrong about this thing that he is pretty sure that God wants. How likely is it that he will see the stoplight or hear "Stop" when he was not willing or able to hear God say "Go"?

Defeating the "Red Light" Strategy with Servanthood

When a person uses the stoplight principle, he either admits he is moving forward without direction or believes God has given direction that he is not able to hear. Does anyone want to be a person who makes this error? Is such a person inviting God to really stop him? Or instead, is he making himself feel more comfortable by including the "option" for God to be involved in his personal search?

Similar to the inappropriate question, this option steals God's glory and demonstrates that a distance already exists between the heart of God and the heart of the wanderer. There is no righteous, biblical example of a man wandering into God's ways. The Bible is abundantly clear; God undeniably reveals Himself and His ways when men choose Him. From the beginning of salvation,

> Keep on asking, and you will be given what you ask for. Keep on looking, and you will find. Keep on knocking, and the door will be opened. For everyone who asks, receives. Everyone who seeks, finds. And the door is opened to everyone who knocks. You parents—if your children ask for a loaf of bread, do you give them a stone instead? Or if they ask for a fish, do you give them a snake? Of course not! If you sinful people know how to give good gifts to your children, how much more will your heavenly Father give good gifts to those who ask him.—Matt. 7:7-11 (NLT)

to needed repentance,

If we confess our sins, He is faithful and righteous to forgive us our sins and to cleanse us from all unrighteousness. — 1 John 1:9 (HCSB)

to intelligent seeking,

Cry out for insight and understanding. Search for them as you would for lost money or hidden treasure. Then you will understand what it means to fear the LORD, and you will gain knowledge of God. For the LORD grants wisdom! From his mouth come knowledge and understanding. — Prov. 2:3-6 (NLT)

even to reading His Word,

All Scripture is inspired by God and profitable for teaching, for reproof, for correction, for training in righteousness; so that the man of God may be adequate, equipped for every good work. — 2 Tim. 3:16-17

God desires to show Himself, His desires, His ways and His direction to believers long before they ever need to ask a question. He will guide them in all His ways if they will only wait on Him for wisdom and direction. He is a God who directs. Christians need to return God's glory to Him, seek Him, and wait for Him to direct the affairs and procedures of their lives.

A life of servanthood, once again, answers this need in the believer's life. Believers need to follow Jesus' example of servanthood by waiting to see where their Father is working and listening for His specific direction before making any decision. How many strong churches with incredible stories of unity would there be today if believers were certain of God's direction to changes churches? How confident would other believers be in God if believers knew where they were going before they left?

One of Satan's goals is to divide and conquer his greatest enemy—God's church. One of man's greatest tendencies is to be selfish. Serving only God and following His truth are the quintessential solutions to problems that divide the church and create poor departures.

Breaking a Cycle of Poor Departures

There is an observable pattern of people leaving poorly. People who leave churches poorly, intentionally or unintentionally, tend to follow the same cycle from arrival to departure at church after church. This three-phase cycle includes the initial excitement phase, the indigenous phase, and the superior phase. The pattern is predictable because it is based on one truth:

People who leave poorly have lived poorly in the church.

The solution the end to this cycle of poor departures is believers living well in the church. Many believers have done just this and are living full and meaningful, long-term, involved relationships with other believers. They have learned the strength of difference. They have learned the beauty found in the variety of ages. They have learned that change can change them for the better. They have learned to love as a commitment. These believers have listened to God's great truths.

However, until a Christian finds the fulfillment of his salvation in heaven, he will be capable of forgetting the great truths and warnings given by God. This reason warrants a look into the details of cycle of poor departures.

The Initial Excitement Phase

The initial excitement phase for the one leaving poorly feels much like the feelings experienced when you fall in love every other month in high school. This phase has the same feeling a young man feels when he meets the new girl in college. It has the same feeling she felt when they got engaged. Honeymooners live in this same initial excitement phase. Everything is better. Everything is prettier. Everything is newer or grander. Churches good at fostering the initial excitement phase are great at building momentous church growth because honeymooners try to get everyone married. They are excited. The unselfish new member is excited about what he will be able to do at this new place. He is looking at new opportunities where he can use what God has given him. He looks for the place to serve or teach and champs at the bit, nearly unable to wait to get the work. New members with a consumer mentality survey the same landscape and see the fun and learning to be had by their family. They are likely to be heard saying things like,

- "The kids love it."
- "Look at that coffee bar."
- "It is so moving."
- "How could you not be excited?"
- "The place is awesome. The building is great."
- "They really have it going on here!"
- "There are tremendous things here that will bless my family."

New people should be excited about new places; it is good. There should be many opportunities of involvement, service, and blessing for both new and old members. It isn't a sin to enjoy church, but it is immature and unhealthy for enjoyment to be a primary reason for going to a church. In the life of the one leaving poorly, the honeymoon will end, and he will face a choice: execute his next move to the next newest thing or enter the indigenous phase.

The Indigenous Phase

There are different maturities and personality types among those who leave poorly. The less mature or more shallow may leave their newest church when the honeymoon ends. The more mature or giving person who leaves poorly will most likely stay and enter the indigenous phase and begin to settle in or become more involved at the church. This is the second phase in the cycle of poor departures.

In the smaller church, a person may be highly involved and attend pretty much as expected. In the large church, he may fade into the crowd, hopefully plugging in to the ministries matching his desires. For most, there is an identity and emptiness to fulfill that can only be fulfilled by being at a new place. Friendships are made, and families enter into commitments. Events are attended, fun is had, and it appears he has finally found the right place. If he is natural leader, he is teaching, building a following, and serving in increasingly key roles in addition to simply being involved in the fellowship. Most of those who leave poorly are genuinely neat people. They are good people. Their greatest weakness may be a misunderstanding of the purpose of church. For whatever reason, most people who leave poorly are simply unknowingly unknowing. In fact, most of them are truly committed during the indigenous phase because they don't intend to leave, don't want to leave, and don't even realize that they have a propensity for leaving poorly. The one prone to poor departure usually does not know of his own ailment.

Some people in the indigenous phase have a consumer mentality. They go to church for what the church is like.

They are part of the fellowship for what it does for or adds to their family. The consumer takes, not because he is greedy, but because he believes that the church exists to serve him or his family. This type of member finds himself attending the meetings and functions that fit him as he customizes his church experience. If he wants friends, he will make them. If he wants simple conversation, he will have it. He may try each new ministry the church promotes. He will gobble up the new culture and take advantage of all the opportunities offered to him as long as those opportunities are more attractive than other things in his life.

Society often views those who give as mature and focused, but the person who is inclined to serve can leave poorly, arrive poorly, and stay in the indigenous phase. These servants will not focus on what their new church does for them but what they can do for their church. The servant finds identity and purpose, and, unfortunately at times, self-worth in serving others. The servant will commit to the place, the idea, and the work of the new church at the same great level he has always committed to every place and their ideas and work. He is by nature a giver and will have many ideas of his own and ideas gathered from previous ministries. Some of those ideas will bring light to the new church. Unfortunately, his commitment to the place, the idea, and the work will be mistaken as a commitment to the people and the body of Christ.

The committed will begin to identify the unhealthy consumer members as the indigenous phase continues. The consumer will only commit to the overall vision and work as long as it interests or benefits him. He is the guy who uses the toilet paper but never puts in a new roll. He may not even give enough offering to pay for the amount he uses. "It is good to have paper, but it isn't my job to stock it," he says.

Time has a way of showing all things:

For each tree is known by its own fruit.—Luke 6:44

and the indigenous phase will end if these consumers are challenged.

The consumer stays based on the relevance of the ministry to his life and desires. The servant may stay indefinitely in a church that allows him to serve on his own terms. However, the person who leaves poorly will enter the third phase of the cycle of poor departures if he is challenged to change. This new phase begins when the church challenges the consumer to become a healthy part of the fellowship or challenges the serving person to serve in another way or doesn't allow him to serve.

The Superior Phase

The third and final phase, the Superior Phase, is the most difficult in the cycle of poor departures. The one who leaves poorly usually begins to construct a justification for his departure during the superior phase. If the fellowship ideas and ways are correct, then he must admit that he is wrong. He has to make his view superior to the views of the fellowship or his friends in order to justify his impending poor departure.

No church is perfect. No person leaving poorly is totally wrong. People who leave poorly may be better at certain things. They may be more mature. The church might not be great at living like a true fellowship. There might be ten good reasons to leave, but the one who leaves poorly will not leave for the one great reason. In the superior phase, the consumer will rarely claim to be superior but will usually claim that the place to which he is going is superior. The servant, having bound himself by service to the fellowship and some of its people, will have to construct a justification.

When the consumer becomes uncomfortable being challenged to go deeper and to be involved in a community, he will probably disappear. The consumer simply says, "This isn't doing it for me anymore. Did you see that new church? They have the best *whatever!*" He probably does not judge his current church. He probably says, "I am not judging. I am just observing." It is unfortunate that the consumer who leaves poorly has not understood the beauty of being part of a community of believers. He is not really part of the church. He is only a consumer and simply needs more than the current church can offer. He can be heard saying, "I need something deeper; I can't learn here" as he searches for a new church and a new beginning to the cycle.

The servant or leader type with a history of leaving poorly usually seems like a part of the heart and soul—the core—of the entire ministry. He seems happy and like family. Then all of the sudden, he is discontent, judgmental, and no longer happy. Many times, even he cannot put his finger on what is wrong. Everything and nothing is wrong all at the same time. He is hurt and does not want to leave, but things have to change. He might catch himself saying,

- "Things just aren't right."
- "Things aren't fair. They aren't being fair."
- "Do they know what they are doing?"
- "I thought they did…"

…without realizing that he is now saying "they" instead of "we." When a servant or leader type moves from the indigenous to superior phase, people in the church often ask about this person:

- What did we do?
- What didn't we do?
- What changed all of the sudden?

- How did this happen?
- How did we miss this?

How does the superior phase come about? Has the church really changed? Is the other church really better? Should the church have changed more to meet the needs of the people? What makes a perfectly content servant or consumer become unhappy, discontent, and departing?

The beginning of the superior phase might be marked by many events. It could be the carpet. It could be the change in teachers or staff. It could be the new leader that the servant has to serve. It might be the young guy who now leads their area of ministry. It might be a change in programs or moving from small groups to Sunday school. It might be a lot of things. It could be a tough series of messages on selfishness and the duty of the member to the church. It could be a call to holiness. It could be asking the giver to step aside so another can teach for a while. It could be the dissolution of the program. It could be pressure put on the consumer to do his turn in the nursery, like everyone else. For the consumer, the superior phase often begins with that challenge to go deeper or with a program change that made the ministry irrelevant to his desires. For the servant or leader type, the consumer phase often begins with a structure or ministry change that affects or demands change in his service or ministry.

Whatever the cause, there is one, common underlying factor: disconnection. The person entering the superior phase does not see himself as part of a family who has made a "better or worse" commitment. This disconnection from the fellowship's values and vision combined with spiritual immaturity leads to a superiority complex. The one who is preparing to leave poorly will find himself justified, the church lacking, and other churches full of great ministries and opportunities. It is a difficult time for him, but also it is clear to him that this church is no longer the place to attend.

Unfortunately, each poor departure decreases the likelihood that the one leaving will connect with the next fellowship. Each poor departure increases the probability that he will leave the next church or just stop attending church. It is like the man who has been married many times. With each marriage the likelihood of his true happiness decreases, and the likelihood of another divorce increases. The end to the cycle will be settling for a final, placating marriage, living alone, or a change in method. The person seasoned in poor departures does not want to be alone but may not be able to accept that he simply isn't good at "doing church." Then again, perhaps he knows he is no good at church relationships, but he is just too tired to change.

The servant or leader type faces the worst challenges in this phase. He is most likely involved in some sort of leadership at this point. He has gotten deeply involved, and as he begins to live through the trials of the family, he finds himself judging people for their failures and weaknesses. He is incapable of assuming any portion of the fault because of the nature of his weakness. He came to find something better, and it does not seem to be there anymore.

The most honorable person trapped in the superior phase will hate leaving and will try to leave without creating division but will position themselves as superior to the church family in the end. It is reminiscent of the 18-year-old son who disavows all allegiance to, and the intelligence of, his father. It is not logical; it is emotional. Even if there are challenges in the church, only the emotional person abandons a family in such need instead of staying to help.

Most who leave poorly are doomed to repeat their previous errors. It is cyclical. It is inevitable. It is seasonal. They may consistently leave in the first or second phases. They may leave poorly once a year, with a year off in between churches. They may leave on a decade cycle. They look like the family, but in the end they will leave the family. They do not live well, so they do not leave well. There is only one hope—a change of method.

Hope Found in a Change of Method

All types of people leave well. The rich, the poor, the highly educated, the less educated, the serious, the happy, the deep, and the shallow can all leave well. Leaving well, like leaving poorly, is indiscriminate of age, sex, or creed.

The common denominator among people who leave poorly is disconnection. The common denominator found in the people who leave a church well is this:

People who leave well will always choose God and His people over themselves.

People who leave well leave honoring, respecting, reconciling, and "going the second mile" (Matt. 5:41-42) with the people of their church. They do this whether the situation they are leaving is blessed or tumultuous, wonderful or terrible. This key to understanding leaving well is to understand that it will always follow the teaching "Love the Lord your God with all your heart, soul and mind and love your neighbor as yourself."

Comedian Flip Wilson used to do a skit where he claimed innocence for all wrong by proclaiming, "The devil made me do it!" Like all good comedy, people laughed again and again at this ridiculous denial of fault because they could identify with it. People are without a doubt creatures of choice. Choice defines humankind and separates people from all else in creation. Christians are enlightened and self-aware and cannot avoid their responsibility when choosing to leave their church. If a Christian leaves a local church poorly, he is responsible. The Christian cannot find himself innocent because, even when influenced by evil, he has pledged himself to only do what God wants him to do.

People who leave a church well make a conscious choice to leave well. They choose to be family. They choose to honor their commitments, whether or not anyone in the church they are leaving honors those commitments. They submit to the leaders because the leaders are the leaders God placed (or at worst, allowed) in their church. They do right because they have a history of choosing right.

The people who leave a church family well are the ones who have learned from God how to live well in a church family. They have learned and now understand how God designed the body of Christ, the church. They have learned the role of the individual. They have learned the importance of true unity and have not settled for consensus. These people who leave well grasp the idea of one Spirit giving one answer to the people who are bound together in the local church. People who leave well know long before their departure how to live well.

There is no simpler way to answer "Why do they leave well?" than to say, "People who leave well have lived well." The cycle of poor departures can be broken with a change of method. People can choose to live well in the fellowship of believers. The next chapter looks at eight characteristics of living well that are found in the lives of believers who live well long before they ever leave well.

Chapter 5

Living Well Before Leaving Well

People who leave well have lived well together. People who leave well live well with their Father God. People who leave well are well—that is, healthy. These people have committed themselves to healthy spiritual living. Though there are many characteristics found among maturing believers, the following are always found in those that leave well. These characteristics are the legs on which the new method of living rests. The new method is the only hope for leaving well.

They Are All on a Great Journey with Their Church

The greatest difference between one who leaves well and one who leaves poorly is his proven track record and current life. A person who leaves well will always be serving God at his current ministry. A person who leaves well will always have a long and current record of:

- being productive and adding to the depth and work of the ministry of his church.
- being called and completing the things he says God calls him to do.
- being united with the fellowship.

- being fully committed to attending, giving to, and serving in the church.
- growing in the Word, individually and corporately.
- hearing from God and others, seeing that truth or fulfillment of what he heard.
- actively and obediently praying.

Someone who leaves well is someone who is connected to the people and the fellowship of his church.

Some of us are Jews, some are Gentiles, some are slaves, and some are free. But we have all been baptized into Christ's body by one Spirit, and we have all received the same Spirit. Yes, the body has many different parts, not just one part. If the foot says, "I am not a part of the body because I am not a hand," that does not make it any less a part of the body. And if the ear says, "I am not part of the body because I am only an ear and not an eye," would that make it any less a part of the body? Suppose the whole body were an eye—then how would you hear? Or if your whole body were just one big ear, how could you smell anything? But God made our bodies with many parts, and he has put each part just where he wants it. What a strange thing a body would be if it had only one part! Yes, there are many parts, but only one body.— 1 Cor. 12:13-20 (NLT)

He is an active saint, with a healthy Christian walk, who is above reproach at his current church. The people of his church know him to be consistent, caring, fair, reliable, steady, mature, selfless, and well-schooled in the Word of God. He has a history of hearing from God—a proven history. He is not flaky, flippant, or inconsistent.

The one who leaves well moves to the next church or ministry because it is the next step in his journey of glorifying God, serving, God and achieving the work of God. In order for this to be true, he has to have been on a productive journey before the call to the next place. He knows it is not about him, his family, or his friends but about God's desire and his service to Him.

They Understand Servanthood

Christians are servants of the Most High—willing slaves who listen for the next command once the last command has been accomplished, never bothering the Master with questions about what is next. These servants know that in God's grace their Master will speak to them, walk with them, and reveal to them what they need to know each day. They understand that there is no begging needed with their God. If they choose Him daily, He will disclose His will to them daily.

> But when He, the Spirit of truth, comes, He will guide you into all the truth; for He will not speak on His own initiative, but whatever He hears, He will speak; and He will disclose to you what is to come. He will glorify Me, for He will take of Mine and will disclose it to you. All things that the Father has are Mine; therefore I said that He takes of Mine and will disclose it to you. —John 16:13-15

These servants understand that when they chose God's way, they chose Him according to Romans 10:

> If you confess with your mouth Jesus as Lord, and believe in your heart that God raised Him from the dead, you will be saved; for with the heart a person believes, resulting in righteousness, and with the

mouth he confesses, resulting in salvation. — Rom. 10:9-10

They know the term "Lord" is not just a name but a term meaning "He is Master" and not a "genie in a lamp." Those who leave well know their God as all-knowing, all-powerful and all-capable to direct them to the next step at the right time. Even when He speaks to their heart as friend or Father, they respect Him and do not trouble Him with repeated questions about the future.

These people understand servanthood and love their role. They read this passage in Mark:

> For even I, the Son of Man, came here not to be served but to serve others, and to give my life as a ransom for many. — Mark 10:45 (NLT)

and understand Jesus did not come to do something or to serve men. Jesus came to serve God on earth. The one who leaves well has lived a life that is all about being a servant of God. He is neither concerned with doing service, nor is he concerned with serving men. His only claim to biblical success is to be a servant of God. He is happy, a bondservant delighting in simply awaiting the Master's voice, whether it be of direction, instruction, correction, or edification.

He does not look at church as a place where he gets but a place where he lives and gives himself to God. He would lay down his life to ransom his local church. He would do anything, suffer everything, to make the church the place it should be for the Master's glory and the betterment of believers.

He has a long record of leaving only when the Master says, "Go here and do…" He does not need to search because He knows that God leads specifically. He is a servant submitted to God's ways, which provide confirmation and direction.

They Understand Submission

Long before they leave, people who leave well understand submission to the saints and to the authority structure of the church. They will never abandon God by disobeying His command to follow earthly leaders. They will never disrespect those same leaders. People who leave well are humble and trust God to vindicate them, if necessary, before the congregation or the leaders. They follow the church's earthly leaders. They answer to the congregation because they understand the biblical model of corporate accountability.

You younger men, accept the authority of the elders. And all of you, serve each other in humility, for "God sets himself against the proud, but he shows favor to the humble." So humble yourselves under the mighty power of God, and in his good time he will honor you. Give all your worries and cares to God, for he cares about what happens to you. Be careful! Watch out for attacks from the Devil, your great enemy. He prowls around like a roaring lion, looking for some victim to devour. Take a firm stand against him, and be strong in your faith. Remember that your Christian brothers and sisters all over the world are going through the same kind of suffering you are.— 1 Pet. 5:5-9 (NLT)

Obey your leaders and submit to them, for they keep watch over your souls as those who will give an account. Let them do this with joy and not with grief, for this would be unprofitable for you.—Heb. 13:17

The person who leaves well remembers how he came. He made a commitment to be in fellowship and appealed to the congregation for confirmation. He said, "I am here," and awaited a confirmation. The person who leaves well really desires this same blessing as he takes the next step in God's journey. He wants the body of Christ to be able to celebrate with him. Even if his current church situation is terrible, he will still appeal to the leaders to anoint his departure, to pray with him, and to bless him.

He understood submission while he grew in the church and continues to embrace it as God calls him to the next place. He is willing to stay if the church recommends he stay. He considers the testimony of his brothers and sisters to be of great value because of their joint commitments made previously. He knows he cannot leave well without a blessing from the church, or at least without trying to obtain that blessing.

They Are Content

One of the greatest but most misused passages in the Bible is Philippians 4:13: I am able to do all things through Him who strengthens me.

This passage has been used to champion basketball teams and to claim "we can do it" when the odds are against us. Thousands of banners and ministry bylines have included the quote or the reference. Ultimately, those uses are simultaneously correct and incorrect. Christians can do all things through Christ who strengthens them, if indeed He strengthens them to do a specific task. But a person cannot claim that he is strengthened to do anything or all things. The Bible teaches that not everyone receives the same gifts, talents, or callings. Though God can clearly gift anyone to do everything, it is dangerous to think that everyone can "do all things."

Now concerning spiritual gifts, brethren, I do not want you to be unaware... Now there are varieties of gifts, but the same Spirit. And there are varieties

of ministries, and the same Lord. There are varieties
of effects, but the same God who works all things
in all persons. But to each one is given the mani-
festation of the Spirit for the common good. For to
one is given the word of wisdom through the Spirit,
and to another the word of knowledge according to
the same Spirit; to another faith by the same Spirit,
and to another gifts of healing by the one Spirit, and
to another the effecting of miracles, and to another
prophecy, and to another the distinguishing of spirits,
to another various kinds of tongues, and to another
the interpretation of tongues. But one and the same
Spirit works all these things, distributing to each one
individually just as He wills. — 1 Cor. 12:1-11

Philippians 4:13 was not claiming that any Christian
could do anything. Its true meaning, the greatness of this
verse, is found while reading it in context.

I don't say this out of need, for I have learned to be
content in whatever circumstances I am. I know both
how to have a little, and I know how to have a lot. In
any and all circumstances I have learned the secret of
being content — whether well-fed or hungry, whether
in abundance or in need. I am able to do all things
through Him who strengthens me. Still, you did well
by sharing with me in my hardship. — Phil. 4:11-14

The context of the verse is contentment in times of wealth
and poverty, plenty and want, and being well-fed and being
hungry. The context is Paul can "do hunger or food, wealth
or poverty…" through Christ who strengthens (gives grace
to) him.

The ones who live and leave well are content in a church
of trial or a church of joy, of plenty or of want. They are

content in a church that is mature or immature, modern or old-fashioned, because Christ gives them grace. They are at their church because they are called to be there. They are mature, and they are on a God-sized mission. The one who leaves well has been around and knows a trial is not always a foe. He knows the mature need to stay in trial and help the immature. He is also great at being content and mature in the good times without forgetting God. He knows it is not about him. He is content to be where God has called him to be.

Content does not always mean we are pleased with the circumstances. Who would be pleased with hunger, poverty, or not getting fed spiritually? Who would be content with wealth leading a church out of dependence on God? Contentment is the ability to endure all things with joy because of God. Contentment is not swayed by circumstance or other believers.

They Are Not Swayed by Those around Them

The one who leaves well has only one alliance—to God. He will always be found to be independent of personal alliances. They are deep, mature people who rely on God for their security and self-view. They have found God as the only reason to live. They know God as the only focus.

The history of Job is told in the Old Testament. This record of a tremendous trial demonstrates that godly people will choose God in bad times as well as in good times. Job's supposed friends and family gave him a lot of advice and commentary during his trial. There were times when they shook his foundation. They challenged his godliness. They asked, "If you are so good, how can all this disaster come upon you?" There is no record of anyone championing Job and encouraging him. Though Job never left his faith in God, he did, after much toil and suffering, question God's reason for the trial. God reminded this devout follower:

Then the LORD answered Job from the whirlwind: "Who is this that questions my wisdom with such ignorant words? Brace yourself, because I have some questions for you, and you must answer them. Where were you when I laid the foundations of the earth? Tell me, if you know so much. Do you know how its dimensions were determined and who did the surveying? What supports its foundations, and who laid its cornerstone as the morning stars sang together and all the angels shouted for joy? Who defined the boundaries of the sea as it burst from the womb, and as I clothed it with clouds and thick darkness? Do you still want to argue with the Almighty? You are God's critic, but do you have the answers?"

Then Job replied to the LORD, "I am nothing—how could I ever find the answers? I will put my hand over my mouth in silence. I have said too much already. I have nothing more to say."

Then the LORD answered Job from the whirlwind: "Brace yourself, because I have some questions for you, and you must answer them. Are you going to discredit my justice and condemn me so you can say you are right? Are you as strong as God, and can you thunder with a voice like his?"—Job 38:1-9, 40:2-9 (NLT)

It is difficult to go it alone. It is difficult to suffer trial or challenge from those who are closest. The one who leaves well has learned that God is God. He knows for certain that following God closely and trusting Him is always the answer. God is the Creator and King of the entire universe. The one who leaves well looks for God to confirm or deny the words of men. In Job's case, though discouraged by the voices of others, he continued to stand on God's truths. He continued to proclaim and cry to God. It was God's opinion and truth that formed the basis for Job's decisions.

In the end of Job's trial, God spoke clearly about the voices of others.

> After the LORD had finished speaking to Job, he said to Eliphaz the Temanite: "I am angry with you and with your two friends, for you have not been right in what you said about me, as my servant Job was. Now take seven young bulls and seven rams and go to my servant Job and offer a burnt offering for yourselves. My servant Job will pray for you, and I will accept his prayer on your behalf. I will not treat you as you deserve, for you have not been right in what you said about me, as my servant Job was." So Eliphaz the Temanite, Bildad the Shuhite, and Zophar the Naamathite did as the LORD commanded them, and the LORD accepted Job's prayer. When Job prayed for his friends, the LORD restored his fortunes. In fact, the LORD gave him twice as much as before! — Job 42:7-11 (NLT)

God found him approved. Job chose God. The friends, with all their good intentions, distractions, and discouragements, did not speak God's words. Their path was the wrong path. Job was thankfully wise.

The one who leaves well has settled the question as to who is God and who is not God. He may, like Job, experience deep feelings and emotions, but he will not abandon God's call. He is not going to change churches because of what someone else says, does, advertises, champions, or challenges. He is fiercely loyal to God.

The ones who leave well are the ones who stayed well. They are not fad followers. They are not martyrs. They are following only one voice and looking for the next great thing wherever and whenever.

They Look Forward to a Bright Future

People who leave well are often more soft-spoken and quieter about why they are at their new church. They do not spend much time talking about how they got to the new church, because they know there is only one statement they could make. The statement is not flashy or exciting. It is, "I simply followed God."

The person who listened to God well at the previous church is listening at the new church. His attitude is one of "being here because of God is enough." There is no need for explanation of why he left or why he arrived. He is looking forward to a bright future from a bright past.

There is a wise saying in the book of Proverbs:

Good people can look forward to a bright future, but the future of the wicked is like a flame going out.— Prov. 13:9 (NCV)

The one who leaves well understands that everything is spiritually focused on the end of salvation when man meets God. He has heard the words of Peter and understands that a holy life of service to God and for His people is the earth-bound goal.

Everything in them will be destroyed by fire, and the earth and everything in it will be burned up. In that way everything will be destroyed. So what kind of people should you be? You should live holy lives and serve God, as you wait for and look forward to the coming of the day of God. When that day comes, the skies will be destroyed with fire, and everything in them will melt with heat. But God made a promise to us, and we are waiting for a new heaven and a new earth where goodness lives.—2 Pet. 3:10-13 (NCV)

There does not need to be a hope of what great thing will happen now that he is at a new church. There is not much to talk about regarding the old, the new, or the future. He did not bring any baggage from the past. He has been, not simply tried to be, reconciled to all men. He is absolutely clear on what God wants him to do at this new place and is not rushing into anything. From deep within and based on the promises of God, he is looking at a guaranteed bright future.

He knows why God wanted him to go. There is a purpose for Him, not him, in mind. The one who leaves well does not talk about what was wrong where he came from but focuses on serving and worshipping where he arrives. He is on a mission and is receiving a call from God.

Watch over your heart with all diligence, for from it flow the springs of life. Put away from you a deceitful mouth and put devious speech far from you. Let your eyes look directly ahead and let your gaze be fixed straight in front of you. Watch the path of your feet and all your ways will be established. Do not turn to the right nor to the left; turn your foot from evil.— Prov. 4:23-27

He has a healthy, positive outlook on life and is not making those arguments and statements that attempt to justify his departure from his previous church. His attitude is one of hope, excitement, and deep joy. He doesn't live in the past nor does he talk about how he thinks and dreams it will be in the future. He has a solid present and a solid call to the day because he hears from God.

They Know How to Hear from God

If the only great reason to leave is because God directs
the move, then Christians really need to hear the voice of
God clearly. A mistake at this point would be critical and
could set them on a wrong course. Those who leave well
are always people who can say, "I am absolutely sure I have
heard from God." Those live well can leave well because
they know how to hear from God. They have grown through
many phases and have chosen God along the way. They have
recognized the difficulty to identifying God's voice, and they
have mastered listening to Him.

There are seven prerequisites found in people who
consistently hear God:

1. They are Christian. The unsaved can hear God's
   conviction and even be swayed by Him; however,
   considering the content of "being certain of God's
   voice," Christianity is required. The non-Christian
   will primarily hear one consistent direction—"Come
   unto Me!"
2. They want to hear from God. Hearing from God does
   not mean they say, "I want to hear from God" but
   rather, they are committed to doing what they hear.
   James 1:5-8 teaches that the one who believes when
   he hears from God will be given wisdom in abundance. Believing His wisdom implies that one will do
   and follow His wisdom. James continues in verse 22
   by encouraging the believer who hears to be a doer.
   The one who is not sure he will do God's bidding may
   never hear that bidding from God.
3. They regularly study the Word. They have studied it
   before the need for wisdom arose. They continue to
   study it after the need for wisdom. God has shown
   much of His character, His truths, and His direction

through His written Word (2 Tim. 3:16). Many times, people wait long to hear the words of wisdom from God because they have not yet studied Him, His ways, or His directions. The one who leaves well has lived well and has thoroughly learned God's character, ways, and truths.

4. They ask God specifically. They do not forget to ask. They do not "follow their heart." They will not plan their life on the words of man. God can use others to talk to believers, but God often has nothing to do with what Billy Bob thinks God wants them to do. The one who hears well listens to those whom God may send his way and then begins the process of hearing the message directly from God for himself. He knows following one's heart usually amounts to little more than man expecting God to bless the direction that he "felt" strongly about (Rom. 11:33-34; 1 Cor. 1:27-29).

5. They listen. When it comes to seeking an answer from God, the young believer does not wait well for an answer. Quiet time before the Lord, without millions of thoughts of exams, friends, cars, jobs, and lists is a hard thing to master, but he has learned to be patient. The one who leaves well has learned to listen well. He asks the Holy Spirit to clear his heart, calm his feelings, and to help him focus on hearing God (1 Kings 19:12).

6. They look for confirmation inside not outside. They look for God to confirm in their heart and mind that what they are hearing is from God. When in their minds they believe God has spoken, they feel comfortable asking God, "Is it You?" When a person is first learning a friend's voice, he answers the phone and with no guilt says, "Is this Jim?" Many godly people have had to learn what the voice of God sounds like.

Judges 6:11-23 records a great example. A godly man named Gideon was not sure at first whom he was talking to, so he asked for confirmation. He did not ask for a sign confirming what he was to do but rather a sign that it was God who was directing him. The angel of the Lord was patient as Gideon sought reassurance. God never tires of helping man understand and communicate with Him, and God gave Gideon a physical miracle as his sign. However, something also happened in Gideon's heart. God provided peace in both his mind and his heart. Gideon was already pretty sure it was God—after all, he prepared an offering to Him. Then after God gave him a sign, Gideon responded from knowledge. He had seen God's message by proclaiming it, building an altar, and then beginning to carry out God's plan. The one leaving well never looks at circumstance for primary direction. People may say, "Then this or that happened, and I just knew God wanted me to do it" or "If the Lord lets that person ask me, then I will know I should do it." Circumstance is not how God directed people in the Bible. Typically, God spoke through a prophet, an angel, the Spirit, or to a person. He told them His message. Then, and only then, did the circumstances line up with the words of God. Many immature people like to quote the history of Gideon laying out a fleece so God would give him direction. However, Gideon did not place the fleece outside to get direction. He placed the fleece because he doubted what God had already told him, what he had heard, and what he had already acted on. Gideon was scared and looking to God for reassurance. He was not looking for confirmation of God's plans or for initial direction through a circumstance. He had already heard the unprompted direction of God. Now, he looked only for assurance from God.

7. They will not accept a biblically inconsistent answer. They know that God will not tell them anything specific to their circumstance that conflicts with any portion of God's Word. They will not claim that the Bible confirms their direction without being able to quote it and keep it in context.

The one who leaves well listens well and knows the voice of God. Despite the wisdom of many counselors (Prov. 15:22) and the fact that circumstance will eventually confirm God's direction, he settles for nothing less than hearing from God.

The one who leaves well rarely needs to ask if he is supposed to leave or move, because he has been hearing from God daily. He has no need to overanalyze and ask because he has learned to hear his Master's voice.

They Know Why They're Here Before They Go There

The people who leave well know they are on a mission from God. They have committed not to get ahead of God and not to run away. They have committed to stay and to make sure their divine purpose is accomplished. Divine purpose? Yes—divine purpose.

Divine purpose is the greatest part of leaving well. To stay or go is to achieve God's divine purpose. Paul understood this when he wrote,

> For me, living is Christ and dying is gain. Now if I live on in the flesh, this means fruitful work for me; and I don't know which one I should choose. I am pressured by both. I have the desire to depart and be with Christ—which is far better— but to remain in

the flesh is more necessary for you.—Phil. 1:21-24 (HCSB)

Paul knew both living and dying would accomplish part of the divine purpose of God. The one who leaves well does not care how he got where he finds himself in the moment. He realizes the all-powerful, all-knowing, and all-mighty God has been planning each moment for him. In that simple moment of submission, he realizes he has been under the watchful care of God as God disciplined, guided, blessed, and drew him to that place. In that simple moment, he has the opportunity to find out why he is there—to find God's divine purpose for him.

As Andrew Murray said, "I am here by God's appointment, in His keeping, under His training for His time."

The one who leaves well is practiced at answering questions like,

- "Why am I here where I find myself?"
- "Am I here by Your design? Would You have chosen this for me?"
- "Did You have to work around me to get me here?"
- "Why am I here today, and what would You have me do?"

Questions like these help him be self-aware and ready to stay. In being ready to stay for God's purpose, he becomes ready to leave for His purpose. Those who leave well have long known why they are where they are before they are called to go anywhere else.

Chapter 6

It's Time to Leave Well

You have lived well. You have become part of the solution. You have dropped church consumerism. You have risen to the battle to claim the glory of God and to do your part to defeat the enemy's plan. You are committed to following God wherever and always having one great reason: "Because God led me."

The day has come. In the midst of all of this great living and commitment, God has called you. There is no denying it. You weren't looking for it. Perhaps your work is complete, or God is moving you to a new state. Perhaps God has called you into ministry or missions. It's time to leave well. And, well, it is exciting and scary at the same time.

You are certain of God's call. Jesus was nailed to a cross to buy your freedom. You are so certain of your departure that you would allow Jesus to die for your move. You have talked to your family, your church, and the leaders, and everyone senses the same excitement and happy sorrow at your new assignment. The party is planned.

Are there any final truths? Is there any final advice? There are tactical matters, a checklist perhaps, that can help the one leaving well. This practical advice is the summary of the biblical truths already presented and can be presented in three categories.

When people do big things, when people do great things, when people make big changes, don't they spend endless amounts of time making great plans? Financial arrangements must be made. Movers must be hired. Strategies must be put in place. Supply lines must be established. Business plans must be submitted and budgets approved.

Nothing great happens in life without a plan. Even fun things have a plan! Interestingly, some people have greater plans regarding what they will wear and how their hair will look than they have for their departure from a church—a home. Even those trying to leave well often fail to get God's plan after they get the call from God. People can get wrapped up in what God is doing and move so quickly that they forget those who love them, count on them, and are going to miss them. They often forget that there may be less mature or even wrong people who don't understand their departure.

What can be done to help the kingdom of God? What can people do for their brothers and sisters in Christ as they plan their departure? What would the Master have them do, not only in leaving but also in arriving at the new destination? Having a wise, peaceful plan bathed in prayer is important. Here are some practical areas to address in your departure plan.

Make People Aware without Becoming the Center of Attention

There is usually some type of formal welcoming or joining ceremony, announcement, or vote when people get saved, commit to, or join a local church. You accepted this as a good entrance strategy; now make it a good exit strategy.

Who leaves home for college without saying goodbye or getting a ride? Who leaves for a new country and does not have a party? Who heads off into a great ministry without a great and prayerful send off?

Why doesn't the local church vote people on to their next God-called place? Many churches may be too immature, too busy, too large, or too disconnected to know who is leaving much less send them off well. Many churches are performance-oriented and have trouble allowing someone to leave happy. Nonetheless, it is important to say goodbye. It is important to inform the leaders of the where, when, why, and how of your departure. If there are any unresolved issues, this is a great time to gently air them out and seek peace in the kingdom of God. It is important for people to grieve the departure or process it.

The one who wants to leave well needs to see the importance of announcing his departure to those close to him and perhaps to tell the entire congregation about his mission and his joy. If the departure comes after trying to be a stand-up guy or gal in a church not willing to change, he may simply want to tell them about his new mission and ask the church to pray. There is no need to try to make any points, correct any issues, or argue when it comes time to say goodbye. All of that work should have been done long before the goodbye.

The goal of saying goodbye is to show the respect anyone would desire. It is important to respect and honor Christian brothers and sisters. You need to say goodbye to your classes, friends and leaders without creating any division. You need to be able to handle the questions and accountability of your family. Your comments need to spring out of a God-given plan that is solid and well thought-out.

Get over any discomfort and say goodbye. Saying goodbye is good for the kingdom, right before men, and polite, and brings glory to God and the new mission. Saying goodbye and all that precedes it will go a long way toward unifying the church.

Be Patient

Natural law teaches people self-preservation. If it is hot, move the hand. If it is threatening, run, hide, or defend. If it is uncomfortable, shift. Unfortunately, God does not operate all spiritual things by natural law. Everything is not humanly intuitive and natural when it comes to God. God illustrates the differences in His approach throughout the Bible. Here is a sampling:

Let no man deceive himself. If any man among you thinks that he is wise in this age, he must become foolish, so that he may become wise. For the wisdom of this world is foolishness before God. — 1 Cor. 3:18-20

"For My thoughts are not your thoughts, and your ways are not My ways." This is the LORD'S declaration. — Isa. 55:8 (HCSB)

Be careful not to draw conclusions of how, when, and to where you should depart. Do not rush the process and stay put until you are certain that God is ready to move you. Sometimes the calling comes long before the implementation.

You need to leave the timing, the steps, and the method entirely up to God. Do not make the mistake of hearing the direction and then rushing ahead without hearing how God wants you to depart. The one who leaves well knows that God's wisdom is not his wisdom, desires to leave only in God's way, and listens for specific instructions.

Resolve Unresolved Issues

Most of the truths about leaving well can be summed up in this one truth: "The one who leaves well is careful not to bring disease with him!" He does not just resolve issues with others, but he also finds biblical answers and finds healing for himself. He solves his problems, is committed to God, and follows His ways. He does not carry known problems into the new church.

If you are not good at tithing, you need to get good before you leave. If you have secret sin, you need to repent and be consistently obedient before you go to a new place. If you are grumpy, you need to find peace.

It is time for you to go, so get well and practice good prevention. Establish regular habits of consistent prayer, quiet prayer, meditation on God's Word, personal Bible study, and consistent service. Value these inoculations against a host of sinful diseases.

It has been said, "If you find a perfect church, join it and it won't be perfect anymore." The one who leaves well leaves "well."

Have an Arrival Plan

The arrival plan is no less important than the departure plan. The arrival plan is like the first prayer of a new couple or the opening lines of a play; it sets the stage for the new work and sets the tone for a person to live well in the new place. Your arrival plan should achieve the following:

- Introduction to the leadership as appropriate.
- Meeting the spiritual leader of the ministry.
- Being active and involved.
- Cutting the apron strings with the past and buying into the new church's plan.
- Embracing the immigrant status and learning the culture before leading or questioning.
- Meeting people—going where they are and not requiring them to come to you.

- Serving as much as you consume.
- Steady, biblical, generous financial support of the church.

All in all, the arrival plan can be summed up well if you can say "Greetings" with a clear and concise explanation of why you have come and what God has told you to do, and a clear offer of support as you bond with your new family.

Epilogue

The plan is complete. Your head is held high, and your heart is humbled by God's call. You are excited and prepared. You have a blessed life ahead, and the church is better for the time, discipline, and self-sacrifice it took you to leave well. You are stronger for the practice of living well among the other believers, and the church is stronger as well for your discipline and practice of living well among believers. Many people are behind you, and the ones who are trying to live well are content and blessed. God is glorified because you chose to live for Him, to choose Him, and to choose His ways in an imperfect world.

That wasn't so difficult, was it?

Printed in the United States
119413LV00001B/337-345/P

9 781604 777512